3 1160 00105 3771

D1526382

Manning-Sanders, Ruth

    Jonnikin and the flying basket; French folk and fairy tales [retold by] Ruth Manning-Sanders; illus. by Victor G. Ambrus. Dutton 1969

152p illus

    This collection of seventeen tales abounds in rich and poor characters as well as demons and witches, both good and bad

1 Fairy tales 2 Folklore—France r Illus. II Title   j398.2

70W21,808   (W) The H. W. Wilson Company

Jonnikin
and the Flying Basket

The King of the Wolves from
Jonnikin and the Flying Basket

Jonnikin
and the Flying Basket

FRENCH FOLK AND FAIRY TALES

RUTH MANNING-SANDERS

Illustrated by Victor G. Ambrus

E. P. DUTTON & CO., INC.   NEW YORK

First published in the U.S.A. 1969
by E. P. Dutton & Co., Inc.

Copyright © 1969 by Ruth Manning-Sanders
All rights reserved. Printed in the U.S.A.

FIRST EDITION

Library of Congress Catalog Card Number: 76-81720

Contents

The Gold Dragoon

Once upon a time there was a count's son who owned a great flying horse, and he flew off on this horse to serve in the army of the king of France.

That horse and the count's son did great things together in the king's wars, and it wasn't long before the count's son was made captain of the company of the Gold Dragoons. And, after that, everyone knew him by the name of the Gold Dragoon. And the Gold Dragoon we will call him.

So, when the French king had conquered his enemies and peace was declared, the Gold Dragoon, having got leave to go home and visit his parents, jumped on his great flying horse, and flew off.

That horse flew more swiftly than any wind can blow; and before midnight the Gold Dragoon, looking down from high,

high, in the air, could see the marble castle, which was his parents' home, gleaming small as a white rose-petal in the moonlight. Then the Gold Dragoon drew in his bridle, and the great flying horse planed down like an eagle to hover above a little river near the marble castle.

'Ha! Ha!' thought the Gold Dragoon. 'How my father and mother will laugh when I come to wake them in their bed!'

But what was that? Someone crying out down below there: someone crying out piteously, 'Oh heaven help me! Oh heaven have mercy on me!'

And there, seated all alone at the side of the road that ran by the little river, the Gold Dragoon saw a maiden in a white robe, weeping bitterly.

The Gold Dragoon flew down to the road. He jumped off the great flying horse and ran to the maiden:

'Lady, what are you doing here alone by the side of the road at midnight, and why do you weep so bitterly?'

'I am here alone by the side of the road,' sobbed the maiden, 'because I have run away from home. And I have run away from home because my parents have betrothed me to the cruel Master of Night. But oh me, oh me, between sunset and sunrise the Master of Night is all-powerful. And however far I may run, and wherever I may hide, I know that before dawn the Master of Night will find me.'

'Not so, lady,' said the Gold Dragoon. 'Should the Master of Night come seeking you, I and my great flying horse will overthrow him; for never yet have we met with an enemy who could defeat us. Come, I will take you to my father's castle: there you shall be well guarded. Dear lady, dry your eyes and let me see you smile! Wait but a moment whilst I go to water my great flying horse at the little river; and then I will take you to my mother.'

The maiden stood up and smiled. 'Gold Dragoon, I thank you from my heart.'

Then the Gold Dragoon led his great flying horse down to the little river that he might drink. And when the great flying horse had drunk his fill, he and the Gold Dragoon went back to the road.

But the road was empty. The maiden had vanished.

'Oh heaven!' cried the Gold Dragoon. 'The Master of Night has stolen the maiden from me! Alack, alack, what shall I do?'

'Master,' said the great flying horse, 'do you love me?'

'Yes, of course I love you, my great flying horse; so often you have helped me in time of war, and brought me safely out of the pains of battle.'

'Then master, as you love me, lie down under this oak and sleep. I will stand sentinel. Sleep till I call you. When I wake you, you shall have news of the Master of Night and of the maiden.'

The Gold Dragoon lay down under the oak and slept. The great flying horse stood sentinel. On the topmost branches of the oak, the white barn-owls and the long-eared owls were chattering:

'*Oo-i-oo, oo-i-oo, ch-ch-ch-ch!*'

The great flying horse understood the language of the owls; the owls who wake by night and see all that happens under the moon, under the stars, or under the black clouds. So the great flying horse lay down on his side and feigned sleep. But he cocked an ear to listen.

At the top of the oak the white barn-owls and the long-eared owls went on chattering:

'*Oo-i-oo, oo-i-oo, ch-ch-ch-ch!* The Master of Night has captured his betrothed maiden. The Master of Night holds the maiden a prisoner in the Wood of Spells, in a little house, near the Fountain of the Wolf. *Oo-i-oo, oo-i-oo, ch-ch-ch-ch!*'

The great flying horse bounds to his feet. He hurries to shake his master, the Gold Dragoon. 'Master, enough of sleep! I know where the maiden is! I know where the Master of Night has taken her!'

The Gold Dragoon springs up, he leaps onto the back of the great flying horse; with one stroke of his wings the great flying horse carries his master to the Wood of Spells, to the threshold of the little house, near the Fountain of the Wolf.

The Gold Dragoon dismounts and draws his sword. *Rat-a-tat-tat! Rat-a-tat-tat!* Without fear or trembling he knocks on the door of the little house.

No answer.

Then the Gold Dragoon puts his shoulder to the door and bursts it open: there within stands the Master of Night, dark and terrible.

'Master of Night, give me back the maiden!'

'No, Gold Dragoon, you shall not have her.'

'Master of Night, defend yourself!'

Their swords clash. That was a battle! But at last the Gold Dragoon overcame the Master of Night and brought him to the ground.

'Gold Dragoon,' said the Master of Night, 'you are stronger than I am; but if you think to kill me, you cannot do it. I live till Judgement Day, and what may happen after that it is not given me to know. But since you have overthrown me, take the maiden. Depart with her on your great flying horse. Only mark well what I say: until the sun rise I have power to torment you. Speak one word, or turn towards your beauty —and I carry her away where you will never find her.'

'Master of Night, I mark well what you say.'

So the Master of Night brought the maiden from where she was hidden; and the Gold Dragoon flew away on the great flying horse, with the maiden up behind him.

The flying horse sped swifter than any wind that blows: nothing in the world could catch up with him. But the Master of Night had no need to catch up with the flying horse, for he had seated himself on the horse's back behind the maiden; and he bit the maiden with his great cruel teeth until she bled; and he took hold of her with his great cruel hands and shook her till she swayed like a reed in a tempest.

'Gold Dragoon,' cried the maiden, 'I fall! I fall!'

The Gold Dragoon did not speak or turn round. He felt for

the maiden's hands and hooked them through his sword-belt.
But the Master of Night went on shaking her: he shook her
till it seemed her arms must be dragged from their sockets,
and her head bowed this way and that over the horse's flanks.

'Gold Dragoon!' she cried. 'The Master of Night will kill
me!'

Then the Gold Dragoon turned sharply round. What did
he see? No Master of Night, no maiden.

'Ah! Ah Merciful heaven! The Master of Night has again!
stolen the maiden from me! Merciful heaven, where are
they?'

The great flying horse planed down like an eagle to hover above a meadow on the edge of a forest.

'Master,' said he, 'do you love me?'

'Yes, yes, I love you, my great flying horse. So often you have saved my life in the terror of battle.'

'Then master, if you love me, swear to me by your soul that you will never exchange me for another animal. Swear by your soul that you will never sell me, no, not for gold nor yet for silver.'

'My great flying horse I swear by my soul all that you ask of me.'

'Then master, now that you have sworn by your soul, we will alight in this meadow, and you shall lie and sleep under yonder oak tree. As for me, I will stand sentinel. Sleep till I call you. When I wake you, you shall have news of the Master of Night and of the maiden.'

They alight. The Gold Dragoon lies under the oak and sleeps. The great flying horse stands sentinel. On the topmost branches of the oak the white barn-owls and the long-eared owls are chattering.

'Oi-o-oo! Oo-i-oo! Ch-ch-ch-ch!'

The great flying horse understands their language. He lies on his side and feigns sleep, but cocks an ear to listen.

'Oo-i-oo! Oo-i-oo! Ch-ch-ch-ch! The Master of Night has recaptured the maiden. Oo-i-oo! Oo-i-oo! Ch-ch-ch-ch! The Master of Night holds the maiden prisoner in a tower, in a tower of gold and silver on the summit of a rock in the middle of the great sea. Oo-i-oo! Oo-i-oo! Ch-ch-ch-ch!'

The great flying horse bounds to his feet. He hurries to shake his master. 'Master, master, enough of sleep! Up on my back! I know where the maiden is! I know where the Master of Night has taken her!'

In a moment they are flying again under the moon, and still flying under the rising sun: flying over plains, over mountains, over rivers, over seas; flying in the noonday sunlight, with their shadows racing under them over the earth; flying in the moonlight again, with their shadows sweeping dark over the leaping waves of ocean, flying, flying, till at midnight they come to a tower of gold and silver, standing on the summit of a rock in the middle of the great sea. And there the great flying horse swoops down and folds his wings.

Rat-a-tat-tat! Rat-a-tat-tat! The Gold Dragoon beats on the tower door.

No answer.

The Gold Dragoon kicks down the door. There within stands the Master of Night, dark and terrible.

'Master of Night, give me back the maiden!'

'Not I! Not I, Gold Dragoon! You shall not have her!'

'Master of Night, defend yourself!'

They draw their swords. They fight till the walls of the gold and silver tower echo with their blows, and sigh with their heavy pantings. The Gold Dragoon at last gets the Master of Night on the ground. But the Master of Night glowers up with his great eyes and says, 'Gold Dragoon, you are stronger than I. But you cannot kill me. I live till Judgement Day. Take the maiden. But remember that till dawn I have power to torment you. Say one word, or turn towards your beauty—and I shall carry her away where you will never find her again. No, never, never!'

'Master of Night, I hear and understand.'

Then the maiden comes from her hiding-place and gets up behind the Gold Dragoon on the great flying horse. Away they fly once more, faster than any wind can blow. But the Master of Night is up behind the maiden. He bites her with his cruel teeth, he shakes her with his cruel hands till her head spins round and round.

Ah, what a maiden! She endures it all. She does not cry out. The Master of Night sees that he is wasting his time. He draws his sword: now he will strike the Gold Dragoon from behind.

'Gold Dragoon, Gold Dragoon!' cries the terrified maiden. 'Defend yourself!'

And the Gold Dragoon turns round.

No maiden! No Master of Night!

'Ah, ah! Heaven help me! The Master of Night has again stolen the maiden! Ah, heaven help me, where are they now?'

'Master,' said the great flying horse, 'do you love me?'

'Yes, yes, my flying horse, indeed I love you! Have I not sworn to you on my soul that I will never exchange you for another animal? Have I not sworn on my soul that I will never sell you, no, not for gold, not yet for silver?'

'Then master, since you love me thus truly, we will alight down there—down there, where I see a grove of oak trees.'

The flying horse planed down like an eagle. He alighted by the grove of oak trees.

'Gold Dragoon, dismount. Go you and sleep under this biggest of the oak trees. I will stand sentinel. When I wake you, I will give you news of the Master of Night, and of the maiden.' So the Gold Dragoon lay down to sleep under the oak tree. On the topmost branches of the oak the white barn-owls and the long-eared owls were chattering:

'Oo-i-oo! Oo-i-oo! Ch-ch-ch-ch! The Master of Night has again captured the maiden. He holds her prisoner far off, very far off, at the bottom of the star in the middle of Orion's belt.'

The great flying horse bounded to shake his master. 'Gold Dragoon, wake, wake! Enough of sleep! Up on my back again! I know where the maiden is! I know where the Master of Night has taken her!'

The Gold Dragoon sprang up. He leaped onto the back of the flying horse. They are off through the air, faster than any wind can blow. At daybreak they came to a great seaport, and there the flying horse furled his wings and alighted outside an inn.

'Gold Dragoon, do you love me?'

'Yes, yes, I love you, my great flying horse: so often you have fought with me and brought me safely out of the din of battle. Have I not sworn on my soul that I will never exchange you for another animal, no, never, never? Have I not sworn that I will never sell you, either for gold, or yet for silver?'

'Then Gold Dragoon swear to me now, on your soul, that

The Gold Dragoon and
The Master of Night

until the day of my death, and however much I may eat, I shall never lack either of hay or corn.'

'I swear it on my soul, my great flying horse.'

'Very well, master. Go, bid the stable boys bring me here seven sacks of corn and as much water as I can drink. In one hour we are setting out on a great journey, a journey such as no man has made before. Whilst I eat my fodder, run to the town. Buy a pound of dry peas and a gold needle. Hurry, hurry! Buy these things and come back at a gallop.'

The Gold Dragoon ran to the town. The stable lads brought for the great flying horse his seven sacks of corn and as much water as he could drink. When the Gold Dragoon came running back with the pound of dry peas and the gold needle, the great flying horse had eaten all his fodder, and the Gold Dragoon sprang up on his back.

Up rose the great flying horse, up and up: up through the clouds, up till the clouds lay far below them; up past the moon, up beyond every planet, up beyond the sun, up, up, and still up, till they came to the blazing stars of Orion's belt. Up to hover above the middle star of that blazing belt, and then down, down into the heart of the star, and still down into its very depths . . .

At the bottom of the star was an iron castle. The Gold Dragoon dismounted, drew his sword, and knocked at the castle door.

Rat-a-tat-tat! Rat-a-tat-tat!

No answer.

The Gold Dragoon kicked down the door. 'Good evening, Master of Night! Give me back the maiden!'

'No, not I!'

'Master of Night, draw and defend yourself!'

Again they fight; again the Gold Dragoon gets the Master of Night on the ground; again the Master of Night gives up the maiden. Ah, but the Master of Night knows what he will do. He has a plan in his head. The Gold Dragoon shall not escape him!

Will he not? The great flying horse has a plan in his head also. And he bids the Gold Dragoon give the maiden the gold needle and the pound of dry peas.

'Now,' said the great flying horse to the maiden, 'take a hair from my tail, thread the gold needle with the hair, and sew up the lips of the Gold Dragoon.'

The maiden took the hair, threaded the needle, and sewed up the lips of the Gold Dragoon. 'Great flying horse, see—it is done!'

'Good. Now lady, take the pound of peas and stuff them firmly into the ears of the Gold Dragoon.'

'Great flying horse, I obey you. See, it is done!'

'Good! Now both of you up on my back. Let us be off quickly. And come with us if you will, Master of Night!'

They are mounted, they are off; the Gold Dragoon in front, the maiden behind the Gold Dragoon, her hands hooked through his sword-belt, the Master of Night behind the maiden. Up from the heart of the star they fly, and down they fly, down past the planets, down past the moon, down into the clouds, down, down, faster than any wind can blow.

The Master of Night, mounted behind the poor maiden, bites her with his cruel teeth, bites her till she bleeds.

The maiden does not cry out.

The Master of Night shakes the poor maiden, shakes her till her head spins.

She does not cry out.

The Master of Night draws his sword to strike the Gold Dragoon from behind.

The maiden does not cry out.

Then the Master of Night calls up a thousand thousand demons. The demons swarm at the Gold Dragoon's back; flames shoot from their mouths, they stretch out their talons to seize him.

Then indeed the maiden cries out in terror: 'Gold Dragoon, Gold Dragoon, defend yourself!'

She may cry as she will: the Gold Dragoon has his ears

stopped, he cannot hear her. The Gold Dragoon has his lips sewn together, he cannot speak. He does not turn around. The great flying horse goes so swiftly that the demons cannot get ahead of him: some cling to his flanks, some crawl to his head, and these the Gold Dragoon cuts down with his sword. But make him turn round they cannot.

The great flying horse is down out of the clouds now. See, there is the earth beneath them! And see, up over the earth's rim shoot the first rays of dawn. And with the coming of the dawn the power of the Master of Night is ended: he and his legion of demons turn into a grey fog; and the grey fog fades away before the rays of the sun.

The great flying horse flew down to earth; he alighted before the marble castle of the parents of the Gold Dragoon. The Gold Dragoon and the maiden sprang from his back. In no time the maiden had unstuffed the ears of the Gold Dragoon, and unpicked the stitches from his lips. The Gold Dragoon took her by the hand and led her into the castle of his parents.

'Good morning, my mother, good morning, my father! Here is the maiden I have chosen for my wife.'

'Ah dear son, how welcome to us is the sight of you! How welcome is the sight of the maiden you have chosen for your wife!'

So the maiden and the Gold Dragoon were married, and lived happily, none more happily. And the Gold Dragoon never forgot the promises he had made to his great flying horse.

Jonnikin and the Flying Basket

There was a young girl, pretty, pretty, absolutely pretty. She had suitors and suitors and more suitors. She drove them all away.

The girl's mother said, 'Don't you want to get married?'

The girl said, 'Of course I do!'

The girl's father said, 'Then make up your mind.'

The girl said, 'My mind *is* made up. When there comes a king with a gold shield on his back, and when this king arrives to fetch me in a fine coach lined with blue satin and studded with diamond nails—*then* I will marry me.'

'Proud, stubborn girl,' said her mother, 'that will never be!'

But the girl's little brother, Jonnikin, who knew more than a bit about magic, cried out, 'Oh, oh, sister, what have you said? Now such a king *may* come—and what then?'

And, sure enough, next day such a king did come. He came in a fine coach lined with blue satin and studded with diamond nails, and he wore a gold shield on his back. But he was the King of the Wolves with a disguise on him. Only he couldn't disguise his tail, and he wore a gold shield to cover it.

Says the King of the Wolves with a bow, 'Pretty one, will you marry me?'

Says the girl with a curtsy, 'Willingly, kind sir.'

And she gets into the coach to drive away with him.

Says little brother Jonnikin, 'I'm coming with you!' And he jumps into the coach.

Says the girl, 'What, *you*, my scrubby little brother! Get out!'

But little brother Jonnikin won't get out. He drives away

with his sister and the King of the Wolves. They drive, drive, and by evening they come to the wolf's castle; and it's a mighty fine one, standing in a great park. There's a grand supper all ready for them, and they eat and drink. And then the King of the Wolves says to the girl, 'You and Jonnikin can go to bed. I have some friends I must see, so that we can arrange about the wedding.'

And he went outside to join his friends.

The girl goes to bed. But Jonnikin sits at a window, looking out. What does he see? He sees the bridegroom take off his man's disguise and his gold shield, and turn into a huge grey wolf. And that wolf gives a howl, loud enough to burst any-

one's eardrums. And from behind the trees in the park a pack of wolves comes galloping.

And the whole pack formed a ring round the huge grey wolf, and began to dance and sing:

> 'Give us your wife,
> Bring out your wife,
> Give us your wife
> That we may eat her!'

But the huge grey wolf sang out in answer:

> 'Let her get fatter first,
> Much, much fatter first,
> We'll let her get fatter first,
> And then we will eat her.'

And after that, he and all the rest of the wolves went dancing off among the trees.

In the morning, Jonnikin tells his sister what he has seen and heard.

She won't believe him. 'How dare you talk to me like that!'

'Well then,' says Jonnikin, 'let me tie a string to your ankle tonight. When the wolves begin to dance and sing, I'll pull on the string to wake you. Then you can come to the window and see for yourself.'

All that day there was the King of the Wolves, dressed up in velvet and silk, with a gold shield on his back, as fine a gentleman as ever you saw. There he was, making eyes at the girl, and smirking, and cramming her with such delicious food as she'd never seen or tasted in all her life. But after supper, he said again, 'You and Jonnikin go to bed. The arrangements for our wedding are almost complete, but I've still a few things to see to.'

The girl went to bed. Jonnikin tied a string to her ankle, stood at the window, and watched. By and by he pulls the string.

'Come here and stand by me,' says Jonnikin.

The girl goes to stand beside him. There down below she sees the pack of wolves in full dance around the huge grey one; and she hears them singing:

'Give us your wife,
Bring out your wife,
Give us your wife
That we may eat her!
Eat her! Eat her!'

And the huge grey wolf was singing out in answer:

'Let her get fatter first,
Much, much fatter first,
We'll let her get fatter first,
And then we will eat her!
Eat her! Eat her!'

Then the girl knew how she had been fooled, and she sobbed and sobbed. 'Oh, how to get out of here? How to get out of here?'

'Well,' says Jonnikin; 'as for me—your scrubby little brother, as you called me—first thing in the morning I'm off home! *You* must do the best you can.'

But the girl clung to him and cried, 'Ah, don't desert me, Jonnikin! Help me! Help me!'

Now Jonnikin was a good-hearted little fellow. He never really meant to desert his sister: only he was a bit offended at her calling him scrubby. So he said, 'Oh, all right. We'll see in the morning.'

In the morning, there was the King of the Wolves, with the gold shield on his back, and dressed up grand as grand, urging the girl to eat a good breakfast. But, poor soul, she couldn't eat a thing. She couldn't even smile. She had a headache, she said. So Jonnikin, who knew more than a bit of magic, goes and makes a great basket, brings it to the King of the Wolves and says, 'Brother, let us amuse ourselves and make my sister laugh. You put plenty of good things to eat and drink in this basket, and put in plenty of gold and silver, too, to steady it. Then do you and your bride get into the basket, and I'll show you a merry trick.'

The King of the Wolves did all that. Anything to amuse the girl and make her laugh, so she would eat again and get fatter! He put a pile of gold and silver coins in the bottom of the basket, brought out rich food and tempting drinks and set them on top of the coins. Then he gets in himself, and in gets the girl beside him: there was plenty of room in that basket!

So, when they were in, Jonnikin pulled on a cord he'd tied to the basket, and sang out, 'Mount, basket, mount! Go home to mother! Home to father!'

And the basket sailed up into the air. The King of the Wolves laughed like anything; but the basket rocked so in the wind that by and by he called out, 'Jonnikin, I feel giddy! Make the basket come down!'

And Jonnikin pulled on the cord, and the basket floated down to earth. The King of the Wolves got out, but the girl sat on where she was.

'Seems you were enjoying it?' said the King of the Wolves.

'Yes, I was enjoying it,' says she. 'I didn't want to come down!'

'Well then,' says Jonnikin, 'we'll give her another ride. I'll get in with my sister this time, and you, brother, shall hold the cord. But when I get giddy you must pull me down.'

'I'll do that,' says the King of the Wolves.

So he takes the cord and Jonnikin gets into the basket, and sings out, 'Mount, basket, mount! Home to mother! Home to father!'

Up goes the basket, up and up. 'Are you feeling giddy yet?' shouts the King of the Wolves.

'No, not yet,' sings out Jonnikin.

And he cuts the cord.

The basket sailed on. The King of the Wolves ran after it, shouting, 'Come down, come down! Give me my wife!' But the basket sails on, faster, faster, higher, higher. The King of the Wolves runs, runs.

'Give me back my wife! Give me back my wife!'

He shouts, he pants, he races. The basket is getting farther and farther away from him. He took such mighty leaps that the gold shield fell from his back and his tail came out. But in his rage he didn't notice this until he was near the girl's home. And then, as he was taking a leap over some thorn bushes, his tail got caught, and he did notice it.

What to do now? The fine gentleman who came a-courting in a coach lined with blue satin and studded with diamonds, mustn't be seen with a tail! The King of the Wolves had to turn in his tracks, pick up the gold shield, and go back to his castle, to fit that gold shield on again with the help of a looking-glass.

And by that time the girl and Jonnikin were safely home.

Jonnikin told his father the whole story. And the father said, 'Come in, and hide that basket in the cellar. When the King of the Wolves comes, we'll arrange something.'

Now, in the garden of their house was a little summer-house, built of bamboos and thatched with straw. There was a table in it, and a bed. The father set plenty of wine, and a plate of little cakes, on the table. He put fireworks under the table, and under the bed, too. And then he went to stand at the garden gate and watch the road.

By and by up comes the King of the Wolves, a mighty fine gentleman, dressed in velvet and satin, and with a gold shield on his back.

'Hasn't Jonnikin arrived yet with my bride?' says this mighty fine gentleman.

'No, not yet,' says the father. 'Will it please you to wait for them in this little summer-house?'

The King of the Wolves went into the little summer-house. He was very thirsty, and very tired. He drank all the wine, and gobbled up all the little cakes. And then he lies down on the bed, falls asleep, and snores, snores.

The father was listening outside. He heard the snores, he crept in, he set off all the fireworks—squibs, Roman candles, crackers, Catherine-wheels, rockets and all.

Out he runs again: *bang! bang! bang!* Off go the squibs and the crackers, leaping all over the floor, up flare the Roman candles, round spin the Catherine-wheels: *whizz, whizz!* Up fly the rockets, they hit the roof, they fall down blazing: the King of the Wolves wakes up, there are flames all round him, the bed is burning, the walls are burning, the roof is burning, his fine clothes are scorched, his hair is scorched, he bounds to the door, the shield falls off his back, his tail is on fire! He bursts the door open, he runs, runs, runs for his life; he is no longer a fine gentleman, he is a huge grey wolf, and the huge grey wolf is galloping for home, with the hair singed all along his back, and his tail on fire.

So, when he had got out of sight of the house, he went and rolled in a muddy ditch to put the fire out, and then he limped home to his castle, and sent for the doctor.

He never came back to fetch the girl.

And the girl—what did she do? Well, she threw her vanity to the winds and married a pleasant young farmer. She didn't go to him empty-handed. She had the gold and silver out of the basket, and the gold shield as well. She made that young farmer a good wife; and thankful she was to have a husband who didn't want to eat her.

The Antmolly Birds

The antmolly birds were big, big birds; and believe me, they could talk. And they had a little young one they were teaching to fly. So on a time when this little young one could just flap down out of the nest, and just flutter up to the nest again, the parents went off to look for food.

'And don't you stir from the nest till we come back,' said they.

But the little antmolly bird was a restless little bird; and he hadn't been alone more than a minute when he felt bored; so *flitter flutter* with him down from the nest, and *hipperty hop, hipperty hop*—off with him round about, to see what he could see.

And he was poking about here and there when a man came along. So the man gave a jump and caught him.

Then the little antmolly bird cried out:

'He has caught him, alas, has this man, eh!
He has caught the child of antmolly,
Caught him, alas, eh!'

'That's right,' said the man, 'I've caught you, and I'm going
to carry you home. Why not, eh? They say antmolly birds
make good eating.'
And the little antmolly bird cried out:

'He will kill him, alas, will this man, eh!
He will kill the child of antmolly,
Kill him, alas, eh!'

'That's right,' said the man. 'Kill you and cook you and eat
you, my little one. And why not, eh?'
So when the man got home, he said to his wife, 'Wife,
here's a little bird for you to cook for our supper.'
And the little antmolly bird cried out:

'He will eat him, alas, will this man, eh!
He will eat the child of antmolly,
Eat him, alas, eh!'

'What!' cried the man's wife. 'Kill and cook and eat a little
bird that talks like a person! Not I! I tell you no good
will come of it! I won't kill it, I won't cook it, I won't
eat it!'
'Well then, if you won't, I will,' said the man.
And he killed the little antmolly bird, and plucked him.
And the little antmolly bird cried out:

'He has plucked him, alas, has this man, eh!
He has plucked the child of antmolly,
Plucked him, alas, eh!'

'It's no good your talking,' said the man. 'I *have* killed you and plucked you, and now—why shouldn't I cook you?' And he put the little antmolly bird in the oven.

And the little antmolly bird cried out of the oven:

'He has cooked him, alas, has this man, eh!
He has cooked the child of antmolly,
Cooked him, alas, eh!'

'Yes I *have* cooked you,' said the man. 'And now—why shouldn't I eat you?'

Then the man ate up the little antmolly bird. And the little antmolly bird cried out of the man's stomach:

'He has eaten, alas, has this man, eh!
He has eaten the child of antmolly,
Has eaten, alas, eh!'

'Be quiet!' said the man. And now that he was full, he went to lie down on his bed.

Now the mother and father antmolly birds—those big, big birds—had come back to the nest; and when they found their little one gone, they set out looking for him. And they were flying around near the man's house, and calling, and calling:

'Gone where is the child of antmolly,
Gone where is the child of antmolly,
Gone where, eh?'

And the little antmolly bird answered out of the man's stomach:

'He is in the man's stomach, alas, eh!
He is here, is the child of antmolly,
Here, here, here!'

Then the mother and father antmolly birds—those big, big birds—broke through the window of the room where the man lay sleeping. They flew to perch on the man's stomach, and they bounced up and down, bounced, *bounced,* BOUNCED with their big feet on the man's stomach, till the man gave a great hiccup, and the little antmolly bird shot out of his mouth.

So then the mother antmolly bird, and the father antmolly bird, took their little one back to the nest. The man lay and groaned: those big, big birds had bruised him sorely. And the man's wife said, 'Serve you right! Didn't I tell you no good would come of killing and eating a little bird that talks like a person?'

The King of the Crows

There was, there was not, and yet somewhere there was a man green as grass, with only one eye, and that eye in the middle of his forehead. This Green Man had three daughters. The eldest was beautiful, the second was more beautiful, but the youngest, who was only ten years old—she was the most beautiful of the three of them.

So one winter evening, the Green Man sat at his window, and outside it was all dark, dark and foggy. And there came a noise of great wings: a bird, big as a bull and black as the pit, flew out of the fog and came to perch on the window-sill.

'*Cou-ack! Cou-ack! Cou-ack!* I am the King of the Crows.'

'King of the Crows, what do you want of me?'

'*Cou-ack! Cou-ack! Cou-ack!* I want one of your daughters in marriage.'

'King of the Crows, wait for me there.'

The Green Man went into the room where his daughters were playing and singing.

'My daughters, listen! The King of the Crows has come. He wants one of you three in marriage.'

Then the eldest daughter spoke up: 'For a whole year I have been engaged to the son of the King of Spain. Yesterday he sent me a message to say that he is coming very soon to take me to his country. So you see, father, I can't marry the King of the Crows.'

And the second daughter said, '*I* am engaged to the Prince of the Isles of the Sea. Yesterday he sent me a message to say that he is coming soon to make me his wife. So you see, father, it is not possible for me to marry the King of the Crows.'

Then the Green Man looked at his youngest daughter—so little, so pretty, so very, very young—and he thought, 'If I should marry this little one to the King of the Crows, I should be forever damned!' And he said nothing to her, but went back to his room.

The King of the Crows was still there, perched on the window-sill.

'King of the Crows, not one of my daughters can marry you.'

The King of the Crows flew into a terrible rage. He dashed at the Green Man, and with a jab of his beak blinded the one eye in the middle of the Green Man's forehead.

'Blind! Blind! Blind!' The Green Man gave a scream, and his daughters heard and came running.

'Father! Dear, dearest father! What has happened? Who has blinded your eye?'

'Ah! Ah!' screamed the Green Man. 'It was the King of the Crows. All three of you have refused to marry him!'

'But father,' said the youngest daughter, the little girl of ten years old, '*I* have not refused to marry the King of the Crows!'

'Oh no matter, no matter! Lead me to my bed. And let none of you come into my room unless I call you.'

Then the youngest daughter, the little girl of ten years old, took her father by the hand, led him to his room, and helped him into his bed.

Next day the Green Man called the youngest daughter to him and said, 'Lead me into the room where I was yesterday when the King of the Crows blinded me. Open the window and leave me alone.'

The little girl did that. The Green Man sat at the window. Night came, dark and foggy. All at once there was a great noise of wings, out there in the fog. A bird, big as a bull and black as the pit, flew out of the fog and came to perch on the window-sill.

'*Cou-ack! Cou-ack! Cou-ack!* I am the King of the Crows.'

'King of the Crows, what do you want of me?'

'*Cou-ack! Cou-ack! Cou-ack!* Green Man, I want one of your three daughters in marriage.'

'King of the Crows, you shall have my youngest daughter.'

Then the King of the Crows stroked the Green Man's eye with a great wing, and gave him back his sight.

'*Cou-ack! Cou-ack! Cou-ack!* Tell my betrothed to be ready tomorrow at daybreak, wearing a white dress and a bridal crown.'

The next morning at daybreak, the sky was black with crows, flying down to the Green Man's house. In front of the house they set up an altar; and in front of the altar stood the King of the Crows hidden under a great shroud, white as snow. When all was ready, and the candles were lighted on the altar, a priest appeared from goodness knows where: the Green Man led out his little daughter, in her white robe and her bridal crown, and the marriage ceremony was held. That done, the priest went away as he had come, and the King of the Crows called out from under his white shroud:

'*Cou-ack! Cou-ack! Cou-ack!* Lead my queen back into her father's house.'

So the Green Man led the little bride back into his house; and the King of the Crows came out from under his shroud.

'*Cou-ack! Cou-ack! Cou-ack!* Green Man, keep your daughter till midday. At midday my crows will carry her to my country.'

And having said that, the King of the Crows flew away towards the north.

At midday the little bride stood on the threshold of her father's house: the sky was black with crows flying down to carry her away. 'Good-bye, my father! Good-bye, my sisters! I am leaving my country, and my home. I am going to a strange land. I shall never come back, never, never!'

Then the crows lifted their little queen on their wings, and carried her away through the air into a cold country: into a country where there were neither trees nor green grass. Before sunset they had travelled nine thousand miles. And then they set her down before the door of a great castle standing on an ice-covered plain surrounded by high mountains.

'Little queen, beautiful little queen, here is your new home. You are the mistress of this castle.'

'Thank you, my crows. I won't forget your service. Now away with you to eat and sleep, my crows, for you well deserve your rest!'

The crows flew away. The little queen went into her castle. It was huge and grand, lighted up everywhere. The hearths blazed with great fires. But she saw no one.

She walked from one grand room to another, and came to a hall where there was a table spread with delicious food and sparkling wines, and laid for but one person. The little queen sat down, but she could neither eat nor drink: so sad she was, remembering her home. So she left the food untouched, and wandered away from the great hall, and came to a room where there was a bed hung with curtains of silver and gold. And she got into bed and lay there trembling, with a lamp burning on a table by her side.

On the first stroke of midnight she heard the sound of great wings. It was the King of the Crows: and he came to alight outside the door.

'Cou-ack! Cou-ack! Cou-ack! Wife, put out the light.'

The little queen put out the lamp, and the King of the Crows came in.

'*Cou-ack! Cou-ack! Cou-ack!* Wife, listen. Once I was a king over men. Now I am the King of the Crows. A wicked wizard has changed us all into birds, me and my people. But I know that our trial will have an end. For that, you can do much. I count on you to do your duty. Every night, as this night, I shall come to sleep at your side. But you are only ten years old. You will not be truly my wife until seven long years have come and gone. Until then, be careful that you never see me, never, never! Otherwise great evil will fall upon me, upon you, and upon my people.'

'King of the Crows, you shall be obeyed.'

Then the little queen heard a soft rustling. It was the King of the Crows taking off his wings and his feathers. That done, he came to lie beside her. The little queen was frightened: she put out her hand, and a kind hand clasped it. Then she fell asleep; and when she woke in the morning, the King of the Crows had gone.

It went on like that for a long, long time. Every midnight the King of the Crows, having taken off his wings and his feathers, came to lie down in the darkness at the little queen's side: every morning, when she woke, he had put on his feathers again and had gone. It seemed to the little queen that she both loved and feared him: and oh, how she longed, longed to see what manner of man he might be! And oh how weary she grew of being all alone, seeing no one, and having no one to talk to!

Often, on fine days, she would pack a basket with food and go out to walk about the desolate country, where the snow lay frozen on the ground and she saw no living thing, not even a black crow or a blade of grass.

But one day, when she was so walking, she came to the foot of a high mountain, and on the top of the mountain there was no snow at all. 'If I went up there,' she thought, 'I might see some grass growing—I might even find a tiny flower!'

So she began to climb the mountain. She climbed and climbed for seven hours and came to the top at last. And there

she found not grass or flowers, but a little hut: and in front of
the hut was an old, old woman, bending over a washing-tub,
rubbing away at some linen that was black as soot, and singing:

'Fairy, Fairy,
Scrub, scrub, scrub,
But still your linen
Lies black in the tub.
None but a queen
Can wash me clean,
Fairy, Fairy!'

You may be sure the little queen was overjoyed to see someone at last, even if it was only an old woman, and she ran to
the old woman, calling out, 'Good day, good day, mother!
Please let me help you to wash that linen clean!'

'So you shall then, poor little one,' said the old woman.

The little queen plunged her hands into the tub; and scarcely
had she given one rub at that linen black as soot, when lo! it
became white as snow.

The old woman laughed and began to sing again:

'Fairy, Fairy,
The task is done,
Spread the white linen
To dry in the sun.
There came a queen
And washed me clean,
Fairy, Fairy!'

So the old woman and the little queen spread out the linen
to dry in the sun. And the old woman said, 'Poor little one,
I have been waiting for you a long, long time. *My* trial is now
over, and it is you I have to thank for that. But your troubles,
poor little one, are not yet at an end. Your husband has given
you good counsel. But what is good counsel worth, since what

is to happen must happen? Now go your way, and come back here only on the day of your greatest need.'

The little queen went back to her lonely castle. One year passed, and another year passed, and more and more years. Until it was now seven years, all but a day, since the King of the Crows had married her on the threshold of her father's house. And the little queen thought:

'I am now seventeen years old. The time of my trial is all but over. One day more, one day less, what does that signify? This very night I will see what manner of man he is—my husband, the King of the Crows.'

So that night she hid a candle and a tinder-box under her pillow and got into bed, leaving a lamp burning on the table by her side.

On the first stroke of midnight came the sound of great wings; and the King of the Crows calling to her from outside the door:

'Cou-ack! Cou-ack! Cou-ack! Wife, put out the light!'

The little queen put out the lamp, heard the King of the Crows come in, heard the soft rustling as he took off his wings and his feathers. That done, he got into bed beside her, and at once fell asleep.

Softly, very softly, the little queen took the candle and the tinder-box from under her pillow. Softly, very softly, she crept out of bed, tiptoed round to the side where her husband was lying, and lit the candle . . .

'Oh heavens, how beautiful my husband is! Never, never could I have believed that anyone could be so very lovely!'

Like one in a dream she stood there, gazing down at her beautiful husband. She forgot everything but that lovely sleeping face. She held the candle nearer and nearer that she might see that face more clearly: the light fell on his closed eyes, and they opened. Ah, he was wide awake!

'Oh my wife, my wife, what have you done? You have brought great misfortune upon me, upon yourself, and upon all my people! Was it so hard to wait just one more night?

Tomorrow our trial would have been ended. I should have
become truly your husband in the shape that you see me. But
now I am going to be separated from all the world. The
wizard who holds me in his power will do with me now just
as he pleases. But what is done is done! To grieve is useless. I
forgive you, my little queen, for the ill you have done me.
Dress now quickly, and go from the castle, where things will
happen that you ought not to see. Go, and may God go with
you, little queen!'

The little queen flung on her clothes and went out weeping.
Then the wicked wizard who held the King of the Crows in
his power came rushing into the room, bound the king with a
huge iron chain, and carried him through the clouds to the
top of a rock on an island in the middle of the sea. There he
buried the end of the chain deep in the rock, and soldered it
with lead. That done, he whistled and two wolves came running, two wolves, big as bulls, the one white, the other black:
the white wolf to watch by day, the black by night.

'Wolves, guard well the King of the Crows!'

'Master, you shall be obeyed.'

The wicked wizard laughed and vanished into the clouds.
The King of the Crows remained alone with the two wolves:
the King of the Crows chained to a rock on an island in the
midst of the sea.

And the little queen, weeping bitter tears, wandered away
from the castle, through the country of frozen snow, through
the country where no one came. And when she reached the
foot of the mountain on whose summit she had met the old
washerwoman, she climbed to the top of it, for she remembered that the old woman had bidden her come back in the
hour of her greatest need.

At the top of the mountain the old woman was sitting at
the door of her hut, spinning and singing softly to herself.

'Poor unhappy little queen!' said she. 'Didn't I tell you that
good counsel goes for nothing, since what is to happen, will
happen? You helped me once, now I will help you. Here are a

pair of iron shoes, to wear as you go seeking your husband, the King of the Crows, a prisoner chained to a rock on an island in the midst of the sea. To free your husband you must find the blue grass, the grass that sings night and day, the grass that breaks the iron. Here is a knapsack in which bread will not be lacking, however much you eat. Here is a gourd in which wine will not be lacking, however much you may drink. Here is a gold-handled knife, a knife to cut the blue grass, the grass that sings night and day, the grass that breaks the iron. When your iron shoes are broken, you will be near to delivering the King of the Crows.'

'Thank you, dear old woman!'

The little queen put on the iron shoes, took the knapsack, the gourd,

and the gold-handled knife, and went down from the mountain. She walked on and on over the frozen snow. In three days she came to a country where there was neither night nor moon, and where the sun shone always. She walked through that country for a whole year. When she was hungry or thirsty she ate the bread from her knapsack and drank the wine from her gourd, and neither bread nor wine was ever lacking. When she had need to sleep, she lay down on the ground, and slept.

And at the end of a year she saw at her feet a clump of blue grass: grass blue as the flower of the flax.

Immediately the little queen took out her gold-handled knife. But the blue grass said, 'Queen, do not cut me with your gold-handled knife. I am the blue grass. But I am not the grass which sings night and day, the grass which breaks the iron.'

So the little queen put up her gold-handled knife and walked on: walked, walked, and in three days came into a country where it was neither night nor day, but where the moon shone always. She walked through that country for a whole year. When she was hungry and thirsty she ate the bread from her knapsack and drank the wine from her gourd, and neither bread nor wine failed her. When she had need to sleep, she lay down on the ground and slept.

At the end of a year she saw at her feet a clump of blue grass, grass blue as the flower of the flax.

The blue grass was singing: 'I am the blue grass, the grass that sings night and day. I am the blue grass, the grass that sings night and day.'

Immediately the little queen took out her gold-handled knife, and stooped to cut the grass. But the grass said, 'Queen, do not cut me with your gold-handled knife. I am the blue grass, the grass that sings night and day. But I am not the grass that breaks the iron.'

The queen put up her gold-handled knife and walked on: walked, walked, and in three days came into a stony country, where there was neither sun nor moon, and where it was always night. She walked through that country for a whole year. When she was hungry and thirsty she ate the bread from her knapsack and drank the wine from her gourd, and neither bread nor wine failed her. When she had need to sleep, she lay down on the ground and slept.

At the end of a year she heard a voice singing in the night: 'I am the blue grass, the grass that sings night and day, the grass that breaks the iron. I am the blue grass, the grass that sings night and day, the grass that breaks the iron.'

Immediately the little queen took out her gold-handled knife, and walked through the dark night towards that singing voice.

Crick! Crack! Clatter! All at once her iron shoes broke and fell off. She had trodden on the blue grass, the grass that sings night and day, the grass that breaks the iron.

So there in the darkness the little queen stooped and felt among the stones for the tuft of grass and cut it; and holding it in her hand walked on barefoot through the night among the stones. And in her hand the grass was always singing, 'I am the blue grass, the grass that sings night and day, the grass that breaks the iron. I am the blue grass, the grass that sings night and day, the grass that breaks the iron.'

The little queen walked on for a long, long time, stumbling through the night amongst the stones; but at last the darkness lifted, and the sun rose. And she was standing on the shore of a great sea, close to a little boat.

The queen got into the little boat, and it sped away with her over the sea. For seven days she saw only the sky and the water; for seven nights she saw nothing at all. But on the morning of the eighth day she landed on the island, and saw the King of the Crows chained on the top of the rock. A great white wolf guarded the king; a great black wolf lay asleep at his side.

As soon as the great white wolf saw the queen, he bounded off the rock and sprang at her, snarling and snapping his jaws.

But the queen held up the blue grass which sang always, 'I am the blue grass, the grass that sings night and day, the grass that breaks the iron.'

And when he heard that song, the great white wolf went back up the rock, lay down at the side of the great black wolf, and slept.

The little queen climbed the rock. She touched the iron chain that bound the King of the Crows, she touched it with the blue grass that sang always, 'I am the blue grass, the grass that sings night and day, the grass that breaks the iron.'

At the touch of the blue grass, the iron chain broke, the blue grass vanished, and the King of the Crows sprang up, strong and well. He flung his arms round his little queen and kissed her many times:

'Oh my little queen, my little queen! You have come at last, my little queen!'

Then the King of the Crows turned to the north:

'*Cou-ack! Cou-ack! Cou-ack! Cou-ack!*'

He turned to the south:

'*Cou-ack! Cou-ack! Cou-ack! Cou-ack!*'

And so to the east and the west:

'*Cou-ack! Cou-ack! Cou-ack! Cou-ack!*'

And whilst he cried thus, thousands of crows came flying from all four quarters of the heaven. And each crow as he landed on the island took the shape of a man. So, when they were all there, the king said:

'Brave people, your trials and mine are over. Look, look down there, down there! It is a king, my neighbour, who comes to fetch us with seven thousand ships.'

The seven thousand ships drew in to the island. The King of the Crows and his little queen, and all his thousands of happy people stepped aboard. They sailed away to their own country: to their own country where the ice and the snow had melted; where now trees grew, and grass, and flowers blossomed, and the air was full of the song of birds: to their own country, where ever after they lived in peace.

The Night of Four Times

Now then, here's a witch, very very old, very very ugly, very very rich. And the older and uglier she gets, the younger and more beautiful she believes herself to be. She has a servant called Bartholomew, and she beats Bartholomew three times a day. She has in a cellar seven barrels of gold, and every morning she drags out all her gold to air in the sun.

So one morning, when she has all her gold spread out and glittering in the sun, up rides a handsome gentleman on a black horse.

Says he to the witch, 'Maiden, lovely maiden, what are you doing?'

Says the witch, 'Gentleman, handsome gentleman, I am airing my gold in the rays of the sun.'

Says he to the witch, 'Maiden, lovely maiden, the gold shines fair. But you, lovely maiden, shine fairer still. Maiden, lovely maiden, will you be my wife?'

The witch's wrinkled face is all one grin. She smirks and giggles. 'Gentleman, handsome gentleman, I am yet too young to marry me. Ride on your way, and come again on the Night of Four Times.'

The handsome gentleman rides away. The witch gives Bartholomew his beating, and carries her gold back into the cellar. A year later, at midnight, the handsome gentleman knocks at the witch's door.

'Maiden, lovely maiden, rise from your bed! It is time to marry us!'

The witch turns in her bed and yells, 'Gentleman, handsome gentleman, what is the weather like?'

'Maiden, lovely maiden, it is raining cats and dogs.'

The witch puts her head out of the window and yells, 'Gentleman, handsome gentleman, ride on your way. I am still too young to marry me.'

The handsome gentleman rides away. A year later, at midnight, there he is, knocking at the witch's door again.

'Maiden, lovely maiden, get up, get up! It is time to marry us!'

The witch turns in her bed and yells, 'Gentleman, handsome gentleman, what is the weather like?'

'Maiden, lovely maiden, it is raining cats and dogs. The storm roars loud enough to deafen you.'

The witch puts her head out of the window and yells, 'Gentleman, handsome gentleman, ride on your way. I am not yet old enough to marry me.'

The handsome gentleman rides away on his black horse. A year later, at midnight, he comes knocking again on the witch's door.

'Maiden, lovely maiden, get up, get up! It is time to marry us.'

The witch turns in her bed and yells, 'Gentleman, handsome gentleman, what is the weather like?'

'Maiden, lovely maiden, it is raining cats and dogs. The storm roars loud enough to deafen you. It blows hard enough to unhorn the bulls.'

The witch puts her head out of the window and yells, 'Gentleman, handsome gentleman, ride on your way. I will not marry me yet.'

So, for the fourth time, a year later at midnight, up gallops the handsome gentleman, and knocks on the witch's door.

'Maiden, lovely maiden, get up! It is time to marry us!'

And the witch shouts from the window, 'Gentleman, handsome gentleman, what is the weather like?'

'Maiden, lovely maiden, it is raining cats and dogs. The storm roars loud enough to deafen you. It blows hard enough to unhorn the bulls. Hail stones fall thick and big round as your fist.'

The witch puts her head out of the window and shouts, 'Gentleman, handsome gentleman, it is the Night of Four Times. Now we will marry us! In one moment I will put on my bridal dress, and my bridal veil that hangs behind the door.'

So the witch dresses herself up like a bride, and then she gives a yell and wakes Bartholomew.

'Ho, Bartholomew, get up, get up! Saddle and bridle your big grey ass.'

'Yes, my young lady.'

'And ho, Bartholomew, stupid dolt,
Saddle for me the ass's colt.'

'Yes, my young lady.'

An hour later, there they go, all three, galloping, galloping through the forest: the witch dressed as a bride, perched on the ass's colt, Bartholomew riding the big grey ass, the handsome gentleman astride his black horse. It is raining cats and dogs, the storm roars loud enough to deafen you, the wind

blows hard enough to unhorn the bulls, hailstones fall thick
and big round as your fist.
    And the witch yells.

> 'Ho, Bartholomew, stupid dolt,
> Whip up, whip up, the ass's colt!'

'Yes, my young lady.'
Bartholomew whips up the ass's colt. On they gallop.
By and by the witch yells again:

> 'Ho, Bartholomew, stupid dolt,
> Whip up, whip up, the ass's colt!'

'Yes, my young lady.'
Bartholomew whips up the ass's colt, and the witch yells:
'Bartholomew, what lovely weather for a wedding!'
'Yes, my young lady.'

> 'Ho, Bartholomew, stupid dolt,
> Whip up, whip up the ass's colt!'

'Yes, my young lady.'
Bartholomew whips up the ass's colt.
    'Bartholomew,' screams the witch, 'do you see those lights
in the wood ahead of us?'
    'Yes, my young lady. They are the eyes of wolves. Their
eyes glow in the dark.'
    'No, stupid Bartholomew,' screams the witch. 'Those lights
are not the eyes of wolves. They are lamps which the handsome gentleman has hung among the trees to light me on my
way. Oh, how rich he is! How he loves me!'
    'Yes, my young lady.'

> 'Ho, Bartholomew, stupid dolt,
> Whip up, whip up the ass's colt!'

'Bartholomew, do you hear those cries in the wood?'
'Yes, my young lady. It is the wolves who howl for hunger.'
'No, stupid Bartholomew, those cries are not the howling
of wolves. They are the songs of minstrels. The handsome
gentleman has ordered out his minstrels to greet me with sweet
singing. Oh, how rich he is! How he loves me!'
'Yes, my young lady.'

'Ho, Bartholomew, stupid dolt,
Whip up faster the ass's colt!'

Bartholomew gives the ass's colt a sharp cut with his whip.
The colt is off at a furious gallop. The wolves are after the
colt. The colt gives a kick and flings the old witch off his back.
There she goes now, in her bride's dress, running for her life
and screaming, with the whole pack of wolves at her heels.
The handsome gentleman laughs and laughs.
'Ho, Bartholomew, will you exchange a bad mistress for a
good master?'
'Yes, master.'
'Ho, Bartholomew, let us ride back to the witch's castle.'
'Yes, master.'
'Ho, Bartholomew, for every beating the witch has given
you, I will give you a piece of gold.'
'Thank you, master.'
So, with the ass's colt trotting behind, they rode back, the
two of them, to the witch's castle, and there they lived in
riches and content.
It is not certain what became of the witch. But two things
are certain: the witch never came back; and the handsome
gentleman kept his word to Bartholomew.

The Little Milleress

A miller and his wife had one daughter, fair as the dawn and good as gold. And every day they sent her to guard their cattle down in the meadows on the river bank.

So, on a time, this little milleress sat spinning at the foot of an old hollow willow tree by the river, with the cattle grazing all round her. And she fell a-thinking:

'Today I am eighteen years old. Soon some fine young fellow will come knocking at our door to ask me in marriage of my parents. Will he be fair? Will he be dark? I don't know; but I think he will be strong and brave and very, very handsome. . . . Perhaps even now he is walking this way.'

Then she looked along the path by the river to see if anyone was walking her way. And there *was* someone walking her way; but it wasn't a fine young fellow, either fair or dark. It was an old man with a long white beard. He had an empty sack slung over his shoulder, and he was hobbling along on a stick.

'Little milleress, I am hungry, and my food bag is empty. For the love of heaven, spare me a morsel to eat!'

'Why, poor old man, I have only some bread and a little milk. But you are welcome to that.'

And she gave him all she had.

'Little milleress, heaven will reward you! Little milleress, shall I tell you what you were thinking as you sat here spinning? You were thinking, "Today I am eighteen years old. Soon some fine young fellow will come knocking at our door to ask me in marriage of my parents." '

'Old man, old man, how do you know that? Old man, old man, who are you?'

'Little milleress, I am John of the Wood. Little milleress, patience. You shall be blessed.'

John of the Wood had scarcely spoken these words when a yell of laughter came from the hollow willow tree. And out jumped a huge man, with glaring red eyes, hair like a furze bush, and skin as yellow as an orange. It was Old Swallowgold, a rascally wizard who ate gold coins for his dinner every day, and who was more wicked and spiteful than a thousand demons.

'Ho, ho! John of the Wood! It is *I*, not you, who will bring the fine young man to ask the little milleress in marriage of her parents!'

When he had said this, Old Swallowgold jumped back into the hollow willow tree. And John of the Wood walked away along the path by the river bank.

The little milleress rounded up the cattle and drove them back to their stalls. And all the way home she was thinking, 'Oh, oh, oh! Something very bad is going to happen!'

That evening, as the little milleress sat at supper with her parents, there came a banging and a stamping on the roof of the millhouse. The fire began to smoke, the smoke filled the room, and down the chimney tumbled a huge hairy man with glaring red eyes, and skin as yellow as an orange. Old Swallowgold!

Old Swallowgold took a little box out of his pocket and opened it. What jumped out? A flea!

'Here you are, little milleress! Here is the fine young fellow who comes to ask you in marriage of your parents. Ho! Ho! John of the Wood took a deal of trouble in choosing him for you. And *when* John of the Wood chose him for you, of all the young fellows in town he was the bravest and strongest and handsomest. But I—ha! ha!—you see what *I* have made of him! Little milleress, I am going to take three hairs from your head; and I am going to hide those hairs where I please. In three days I shall come again. If then you can tell me where I have hidden those three hairs, your flea will become again a fine young fellow, strong, brave, and very, very handsome. But if you *can't* tell me where your three hairs are hidden, well, well, well—I condemn you to marry him as he is now. And as he is now, so he will remain ever afterwards.'

The little milleress burst into tears. But the flea gave a big, big hop, and jumped into her ear. 'Little milleress,' whispered the flea, 'don't be afraid. Leave me to deal with Old Swallow-gold! Let him take your three hairs. Hide them where he will —*I'll* find them! And then I shall become once more a fine young fellow, strong and brave and very, very handsome.'

The little milleress bowed her head. 'Old Swallowgold,' said she, 'take what you must.'

Then Old Swallowgold plucked three hairs from the head of the little milleress, wound them round a chip of wood, and tucked them away in his pocket. But the flea didn't waste his time. He gave a big, big hop, and jumped from the ear of the little milleress into the bush of hair on Old Swallowgold's head. And hidden there, he listened and watched without being seen.

Old Swallowgold scrambled back up the chimney. For the whole night he went walking, walking, away towards the

Old Swallowgold from
The Little Milleress

south. At dawn he came to the outskirts of a town, and there at the side of the road, were three deep dark wells. He looked behind him, he looked in front of him, he looked to this side and that . . . nobody about! He unwound one of the hairs from the chip of wood and dropped it into the middle well.

'Find that hair, little milleress; find that hair if you can!'

But the flea, hidden in the bush of hair on Old Swallowgold's head, listened and watched without being seen.

Old Swallowgold walked on into the town. He came to a big church and went in. There was a pile of chairs stacked up in one corner of the church. Old Swallowgold jumped into the middle of the pile, pulled some chairs over him, and so, safely hidden, curled up and went to sleep.

But the flea stayed awake: he watched and listened.

Old Swallowgold slept all through the day. He had pleasant dreams about the poor little milleress, and woke laughing when the clock on the church tower struck midnight. . . . Now to hide the second hair! Ah ha! He thought of a good place. He climbed up the belfry stairs and tied that second hair round the clapper of the biggest bell.

'Find that second hair, little milleress, if you can!'

But the flea, hidden in the bush of hair on Old Swallowgold's head, watched and listened without being seen.

Old Swallowgold felt hungry. He hadn't had his dinner yet. So he clapped his hands above his head and brought them down filled with gold coins. He swallowed those gold coins and clapped his hands above his head again, and yet again. And every time he brought his hands down, they were filled with gold coins. He gobbled up those gold coins till he was full of them, and didn't feel hungry any more. Then he went out of the church and walked away through the night.

All that night, and all next day, and all the following night he walked and walked. Where should he hide that last hair? He couldn't decide. At sunrise on the third day he looked about him. Well, well, he had been walking in a circle; and there he was now on the river bank, close to the miller's home.

'A thousand devils! The three days are up, and I haven't yet chosen a hiding-place for that last hair of the little milleress . . . Bah! Best way not to hide it at all; best way leave it in my pocket—she'll never guess that!'

So Old Swallowgold left that last hair wound round the chip of wood in his pocket.

But the flea, hidden in the bush of hair on Old Swallowgold's head, was listening and watching without being seen.

Without being seen, without being heard, without being felt, the flea gave a hop and jumped into Old Swallowgold's pocket. Without being seen, without being heard, without being felt, he unwound the hair from round the chip of wood, and tied it round Old Swallowgold's waist. That done, he jumped back into Old Swallowgold's bush of hair.

That evening, as the little milleress sat at supper with her parents, there came a banging and a stamping on the roof of the millhouse. The fire smoked, the smoke filled the room, and down from the chimney Old Swallowgold came tumbling.

'Good evening, good people! Good evening, little milleress! The three days are passed. If you can tell me where your three hairs are hidden, your flea will at once become a fine young man, strong, brave, and very, very handsome. If you *can't* tell me—well, well, well, I condemn you to marry him just as he is. And as he is now, so he will remain until he dies.'

Whilst Old Swallowgold was speaking, the flea didn't waste any time. He gave a big, big hop, and jumped from Old Swallowgold's head into the ear of the little milleress.

'Little milleress,' whispered the flea, 'don't you be afraid! Take me from your ear and put me between your lips. *I* will answer Old Swallowgold's questions.'

The little milleress did as the flea bade her, and kept her lips apart.

'Little milleress,' said Old Swallowgold, 'tell me where I have hidden the first of your hairs.'

'Old Swallowgold,' answered the flea, out of the mouth of the little milleress, 'many and many a league to the south of us there stands a town. On the outskirts of that town are three deep dark wells. It is in the middle one of those three wells that you have hidden the first of my hairs.'

Old Swallowgold gave a yell of rage. How did she know that? How *did* she? He stamped his foot and shouted, 'Little milleress, I defy you to tell me where I have hidden the second of your three hairs!'

'Old Swallowgold,' answered the flea out of the mouth of the little milleress, 'in that same town there is a church. And in the belfry of that church hang seven bells. It is round the clapper of the biggest bell that you have tied the second of my three hairs.'

Old Swallowgold's eyes flashed fire. In his rage he spat out a gold coin, which the miller quickly picked up. 'Little milleress, little milleress,' shouted Old Swallowgold, 'and what about that last hair of yours? Where is that hidden?'

'Old Swallowgold, the last of my three hairs is tied about your waist.'

'You lie, little milleress, you lie! The last of your three hairs is in my pocket!'

'Old Swallowgold, it is *you* who lie. Feel in your pocket.'

Old Swallowgold put his hand in his pocket and took out the chip of wood. He stared and stared. There was no hair wound round that chip of wood.

'Old Swallowgold, as I said, it is tied about your waist.'

'It isn't tied about my waist, it *isn't!*' screamed Old Swallowgold.

But sure enough it was. And what was more, Old Swallowgold couldn't untie it, and it was growing thicker and thicker and longer and longer, till it became a great big strong rope. And whilst Old Swallowgold was struggling to get himself free from that rope, the flea gave a hop, and jumped out from between the lips of the little milleress and landed on the floor.

What stood there on the floor now? No flea, but a fine young fellow, strong and brave, and very, very handsome. And as that fine young fellow took the little milleress in his arms and kissed her—who should walk in at the door but John of the Wood!

John of the Wood seized the end of the rope that dangled from Old Swallowgold's waist, and tied that rope fast to the door-post. 'Come on, my friends, come on!' cried John of the Wood. 'The time has come to teach Old Swallowgold a lesson!'

And John of the Wood brought his stick, *whack, whack, whack,* down on Old Swallowgold's shoulders.

The father of the little milleress seized the poker. And *whack, whack, whack,* went that poker on Old Swallowgold's back. The mother of the little milleress snatched up the fire shovel: *whack, whack, whack,* went the fire shovel on Old Swallowgold's legs. The little milleress seized up her distaff: *whack, whack, whack!* The fine young fellow seized the broom, *whack, whack, whack!* Old Swallowgold writhed and screamed; and at every blow of stick, poker, fire shovel, distaff and broom a gold coin fell out of Old Swallowgold's mouth.

'Come on, my friends, come on, he's not empty yet!'

Whack, whack, whack, whack! More gold coins, and more, and more.

But at last Old Swallowgold had spat up every piece of gold that was in him. He was empty as empty, and thin as a lath; and the floor was strewn thick with golden coins. So then they stopped beating him. John of the Wood untied the rope, and Old Swallowgold rushed screaming up the chimney.

John of the Wood laughed. 'Come, my friends, let us gather up all this gold. It is your dowry, little milleress, and tomorrow shall be your wedding day.'

So next morning the little milleress was married to the fine young fellow, whom John of the Wood had chosen for her: the fine young fellow so strong, so brave, so very, very handsome. And after the wedding, John of the Wood slung his bag over his shoulder, and took his stick in his hand.

'Good-bye, my friends. Live rich, happy and contented. As for me, I must now leave you. I have business elsewhere.'

Then John of the Wood walked away along the path by the river. And they never saw him again; no, never, never.

The Thirteen Flies

There was once a weaver as lazy as a dog. No man ever saw
him working at his loom. And yet the cloth he produced was
the finest in the world; and if he agreed with a customer to
have cloth ready on a certain day, sure enough that cloth was
ready; although there he was sitting in the sun, doing nothing.

He never dug in his garden. He never laboured in his field.
He never worked in his vineyard—and yet every year he produced from his garden, from his field, from his vineyard,
three times as much in vegetables, grain, and grapes as any of
his neighbours.

Oh dear me—how does he manage it? That's what his
neighbours wonder, that's what his wife wants to know. She
pesters him with questions, but he only laughs. She gets angry
and scolds, she gets tearful and pleads—he only laughs. She
spies on him—no good at all. After seven years of marriage
she knows no more than she did on her wedding day.

So one fine morning the weaver says, 'Wife, I'm off to the
fair, maybe to buy some mules. You shall stay at home to
mind the house and have all shipshape by the time I come
back.'

'Never fear, my man,' says she, 'the house shall be seen to.'

So off goes the weaver, sauntering along, whistling and
smiling to himself. The wife looks after him. 'What's he up to
now? Is he going to the fair to buy mules, or isn't he? Will he
come back, not with mules, but with an armful of fine cloth,
got from Lord knows where? Bah!' thinks she. 'Let the house
see to itself! I'm off and after him!'

So out she goes, following her husband, slipping along
behind trees and hedges, lest he turn round and see her. But
he didn't turn round. He sauntered on till he came to a little
wood, and there he stopped at the foot of a juniper tree, took
something from his pocket, bent down, hid that something
under the moss at the roots of the tree, and sauntered on again,
still smiling to himself.

Five minutes later, the wife was scrabbling in the moss at
the foot of the juniper tree to see what her husband had
hidden.

It was a little box. And from the box came a throbbing
and a buzzing, and a turmoil of little voices:

'*Brrr!* Open the box! *Brrr!* Where is the work? *Brrr!* Open
the box!'

The wife hurries home with the box; and all the time she
is going she hears those little buzzing voices, '*Brrr!* Open the
box! *Brrr!* Where is the work? *Brrr!* Open the box!'

Well, she gets home, goes into the kitchen, shuts the door,
puts the box on the table, and opens it.

Immediately out come thirteen flies and buzz about the room, crying, 'Brrr! Where is the work? Brrr! Where is the work? Brrr! Where is the work?'

The wife is terrified, and she screams out, 'Flies, flies, flies, get back into the box, can't you?'

When she said that, the flies went back into the box, quick enough; but still she could hear them buzzing away inside there: 'Brrr! Open the box! Brrr! Where is the work? Brrr! Open the box!'

So she picked up the box, ran back to the wood, and hid the box again under the moss at the foot of the juniper tree.

When her man came sauntering back that evening, he was carrying a roll of cloth.

'Well, did you buy those mules?' says she.

'No,' says he.

'I thought not,' says she.

'I was busy about some cloth,' says he.

'So I see,' says she. 'Well, drink your soup. But you haven't any more secrets from me! I know now who are the workmen who labour instead of you. They are thirteen flies that you keep prisoners in a little box.'

'Well, God bless you!' says he, laughing. 'It's a true word you've spoken. And good little workmen they are, as all the world can see!'

'And is it right and proper,' says she, getting angry, 'that I should be working my fingers to the bone keeping your house, and you should be idling day in, day out, and letting these creatures work for you?'

The weaver laughs again. 'Well wife, if that's how you feel, you shall have my workmen for a while. They'll obey you as they obey me. Tomorrow set them to work, and you rest a bit.'

'That'll be a rare change,' says she. 'But what about *your* work?'

'Maybe it'll be a rare change for me to do a bit myself,' says he.

So early next morning the weaver goes to his loom, and the wife goes off to the wood to bring home the little box. She puts it on the table and opens it. Out come the flies. '*Brrr!* Where is the work? *Brrr!* Where is the work? *Brrr!* Where is the work?'

'There's work a-plenty,' says she. 'Make the bed, clean the house, fetch water from the well, peel the potatoes, wash the cabbage, stoke up the fire, put on the pot to boil, serve me a nice drop of soup, and then get busy baking bread.'

Down she sits with her arms folded. But she didn't sit long. The flies had all that work done before she could count twenty, and there they were now buzzing round her head again: '*Brrr!* Where is the work? *Brrr!* Where is the work?'

She shouts at them to stop bothering. But they won't. '*Brrr!* Where is the work? *Brrr!* Where is the work?' So then she gets desperate and shouts out, 'Get back into the box with you, you varmints!'

The flies went back into the box. She shut down the lid and put the box under the chair cushion. But inside the box the flies were buzzing up and down, the box was quivering and humming, and the chair cushion was all of a tremble. '*Brrr!* Open the box! *Brrr!* Where is the work? *Brrr!* Open the box!'

She lost all patience. She tossed the chair cushion onto the floor, took up the box, opened it, and screamed, 'Well, if you want something to do, take the roof off the house! For that's something you can't do, I'll warrant!'

Oh ho, couldn't they? They had the roof off in a twinkling, and the wind came swirling through the house, and blew everything about her ears.

'Put it back, put it back, *put that roof back on again!*' she shrieked.

And they did. And she bade them go back into the box, and they did. She pushed the box away under the chair cushion, and spent the rest of the day tidying up what the wind had scattered.

But inside the box the flies were still buzzing up and down, the box was quivering and humming, the chair cushion was all of a quiver: '*Brrr!* Open the box! *Brrr!* Where is the work? *Brrr!* Open the box!'

At sunset the weaver came back from his workshop. 'Well, wife, I've done a day's work for once in my life. And how have you got on?'

'Oh, well enough,' said she. Though she felt like crying.

'And did my little workmen save you labour?'

'Maybe they did,' said she, 'but they nigh drove me crazy. And you just hark at them now!'

'Well, wife, you'll get used to that,' says he, and laughs.

Next day it was the same. The weaver went to his loom, the wife set the flies to work for her. They got everything done in a twinkling, and there they were buzzing round and round her: '*Brrr!* Where is the work? *Brrr!* Where is the work?' She bade them go back into the box, and there they were inside it: '*Brrr!* Open the box! *Brrr!* Where is the work? *Brrr!* Open the box!' She let them out of the box again, '*Brrr!* Where is the work? *Brrr!* Where is the work?'

All day long she was letting them out of the box, and sending them in again. And though she did no work, she got no rest. She felt half mad, thinking up things for the flies to do, and they doing it all in a twinkling, and buzzing round her head for more work and more work and still more work.

At sunset the weaver comes back from his workshop. 'Well, wife, I've done another good day's work. But what's the matter with *you*?'

'Those dratted flies!' says she.

So he just smiles and says nothing.

That's the way it goes on, for maybe a week. The wife lies awake at night, thinking of impossible tasks to set the flies. But it seemed nothing was impossible to them. And then one night she has a fine idea.

So in the morning she opens the box and says to the flies, 'Flies, yonder is the river; and here are six sieves, six strainers

and a tub with twelve holes in the bottom of it. Go to the
river; and in these sieves, these strainers, and this holed tub,
bring me here all the water from the river. And don't you
leave one drop behind!'

The flies buzz off to the river. The wife sits in triumph at
the doorway. But—heaven help us!—what is this? The flies
are coming back, and from the six sieves, the six strainers, and
the tub with twelve holes in the bottom of it, a flood of water
is pouring out. The flood comes on and on; it laps about the
doorway; the wife slams the door and rushes into the kitchen;
the flood comes on and on, it laps about the kitchen window,
it streams under the door, it fills the kitchen. The wife rushes
upstairs; the flood comes after her; it fills the bedroom. The
wife clambers through a skylight onto the roof, the flood
comes after her. Now as she stands on the roof, the water is
over her ankles; now it is up to her waist; and swiftly,
swiftly, all the countryside—the meadows, the trees, the
cottages—disappear under the flood. Only the track of the
river is dry as a bone with stones and sand gleaming on its
empty bed.

The wife began to scream then: 'Put the water back in the
river, put the water back!'

So the flies put it back in a twinkling. There again were the
fields and the cottages and the trees all lit up and shining in
the sun; and there was the river flowing peacefully between
its banks.

Then at her bidding the flies went back into the box, but
all day long they were crying, '*Brrr!* Open the box! *Brrr!*
Where is the work? *Brrr!* Open the box!'

And all day long the wife sat and wept.

'Husband,' she sobbed, when the weaver came home at
sunset, 'the flies are driving me out of my mind! Send them
away!'

The weaver laughed.

'Wife, it shall be as you wish.' He picked up the box and
opened it. 'Flies, be off with you!'

But the flies came buzzing round his head. '*Brrr!* Give us our wages! *Brrr!* Then we will go. *Brrr!* Give us our wages! *Brrr!* Then we will go.'

'Flies, over there, over there, in the little wood, perched on a branch of the juniper tree, you will find thirteen crows. Take them in payment for your labour.'

'*Brrr!* We are going! *Brrr!* We will take the crows!'

The flies flew off to the juniper tree. Each one took a crow. Where they went after that, no one knows. They never came back to the weaver; no, never, never.

The Handsome Apprentice

A poor widow had a son, handsome and good. And one day this lad said, 'Mother, I am now fourteen years old. To-morrow I shall go and apprentice myself to the smith who lives by the river.'

'Oh no, my son, oh no! You mustn't think of it!' says she. 'That smith is not a man like other men. He has had seven apprentices, and they all died in three days.'

'Mother, *I* shall not die! Mother, I am going.'

Go he would, and go he did. The very next morning, there he is, knocking at the smith's door.

'Ho! Smith! Ho! Ho! Ho!'

The door opens, out bounds the smith, and doubles up his

fist to give the lad a blow. But the lad leaps aside and laughs.

'Young son of a dog,' roars the smith, 'what do you want?'

'What do I want? That's easy said! I want to be your apprentice.'

'Young son of a dog, come into my workshop.'

The lad goes boldly into the workshop, and the smith roars out, 'Young son of a dog, prove to me that you are strong.'

Then the lad took up an anvil weighing seven hundred-weight, swung it round his head and flung it through the open door. The anvil flew through the air and buried itself in the ground six hundred feet away.

'Young son of a dog, you are strong. Prove to me that you are also neat-handed.'

The lad put up his hand to a spider's web. He took the web between his fingers and wound it into a ball, without breaking a thread.

'Young son of a dog, you are strong and neat-handed. Prove to me that you are also brave.'

The smith opened the door of a little room behind the forge. In the room was a great black wolf that the smith kept to blow the bellows. The wolf rushed out and leaped on the lad to tear him to pieces. But the lad caught the wolf by the tail, flung him back behind the bellows and slammed the door on him.

'Young son of a dog, you are strong, neat-handed, and brave. Come to me in three days' time and I will take you as my apprentice. I will pay you well; but you shall neither eat nor sleep in my house.'

'Master, in three days' time I shall be here.'

The lad went towards home. He was thinking, 'My mother was right. The smith is not a man as other men. For the next three days I will hide myself and watch him, that I may find out who and what he is.'

When he got home the lad said to his mother, 'Mother, we shall be rich! The smith has taken me for his apprentice, and he will pay me well. I begin work in three days from now; and meantime I wish to take a little holiday to look about me. Put me up a knapsack of bread and a gourd of wine, dear mother, and give me your blessing before I go.'

The mother filled a knapsack with bread and a gourd with wine. 'Here you are, my son. And may the good God guard you from all evil!'

The lad kissed his mother and set out, as if on a journey. But did he go on that journey? Not he! When he had walked a little way, he turned back, came near to the smith's house, and hid in a haystack.

At sunset the smith locked up the workshop and went into his house. The lad, hidden in the haystack, watched and listened. Twilight came, darkness came, the stars shone out. At eleven o'clock the smith opens the door of his house very softly, and looks all round him. He sees no one; he hears nothing. He puts his hands to his mouth and calls in the manner of a grasshopper:

'*Cree! Cree! Cree!* Come, my daughter! Come, Queen of the Vipers!'

'Papa, I am here!'

The Queen of the Vipers glides out of the night. She is long and smooth and round as a sack of corn. And on her head is the pattern of a black lily. The father and daughter embrace many, many times.

'Papa, you have a new apprentice?'

'Daughter, I shall have one in three days' time. A lad handsome, strong, neat-handed, and brave.'

'Papa, I have seen him. Papa, he is more than handsome! He walks as if the world were his! I love him, Papa, I love him!'

'My daughter, when he is old enough you shall marry him. But go now, for midnight draws near. I have only just time to get ready.'

The Queen of the Vipers slid away into the night. The mith went down to a meadow on the river bank, a meadow bordered with willows. The lad came out from under the haystack, and quietly, very quietly, followed the smith down into the meadow.

What was the smith doing, there on the river bank in the starlight? He was taking off his clothes and hiding them in a hollow willow tree. And what was the smith doing *now*, as he stood there all naked? He was peeling off his skin from feet to head, and hiding it along with his clothes in the hollow willow tree.

And when his skin was off, there he was, a man no longer, but a great brown otter.

Midnight by the stars! The otter plunged into the river, dived deep, came up with a carp, ate the carp, dived again, came up with an eel, ate the eel, dived again—swam, dived, swam, dived, all the night through. And hidden behind the willow trees the lad watched till sunrise. Then the otter came out of the river, the lad ran to hide in the haystack, and the otter put on his man's skin and his man's clothes.

Now here is the smith walking back to his house, never thinking that the lad has been watching him.

'So,' thought the lad, 'my master is a man by day, an otter by night. My master's daughter is the Queen of the Vipers. She has fallen in love with me, and when I am old enough she intends to marry me. All that is good to know, but not to speak of.'

Early on the third day, the lad came out of his hiding-place, brushed himself clean of hay, and went to the smithy.

'Good morning, master. I have come to begin my apprenticeship.'

Now the smith worked not only in iron, but also in silver and gold and jewels. He was clever, none cleverer; work came to him like hail falling. But the lad was clever, too; he worked hard, he worked well, and when he had been with the smith for a year he knew already more than his master. But he didn't let the smith know that: he made mistakes on purpose sometimes, fearing his master's jealousy.

One evening the smith said to the lad, 'Listen. In three months from now the elder daughter of a rich marquis is to marry the King of the Isles. I have orders to make for the bride rings, bracelets, earrings, necklaces, jewelled girdles, and every kind of costly adornment. In the marquis's castle there is no lack of all we shall need to make these things, no lack of gold or silver or diamonds and other precious stones. I am sending you now to rough out the work as well as you can. A month before the wedding I shall come myself, to see that all is well, and to do the finer work that is beyond your skill.'

The lad went to the marquis's castle. They gave him a workroom. They brought to him gold, silver, glittering jewels, softly gleaming pearls. 'Ah ha! Master!' thinks the lad. 'Now we shall see whether or no there is work that is beyond my skill!'

He set to work. Never had there been seen, never perhaps would there be seen again, such beautiful rings, such magnificent coronets and necklaces, such fine girdles, such exquisite earrings as that lad made. Master, mistress, and servants gathered round to watch his work and praise him. 'Oh, oh, oh!' the future bride was clapping her hands with delight.

Now the future bride had a little sister, smiling, bright, and fair as the morning star. She watched till she found the lad alone, and then she went to him:

'Apprentice, handsome apprentice, you make beautiful and wonderful things for my elder sister. Tell me, and tell me truly, would you make things still more beautiful and wonderful for another girl?'

'Yes, little maiden. If I had a sweetheart I would make for her a collar of gold without its equal in the world.'

'Apprentice, handsome apprentice, what would it be like, this collar of gold that you would make for your sweetheart, this collar of gold without its equal in the world?'

'For my sweetheart, little maiden, I would make a collar of gold, a beautiful collar of yellow gold, shining like the sun.

The smith from *The Handsome Apprentice*

This collar I would temper in the burning coals on my forge; I would take it out all hot, I would cut my arm and let my blood flow over it; then I would temper it again in the burning coals, and whilst it was still warm, I would fasten it round my sweetheart's neck. It would become one with her flesh, so much so that no power in heaven or earth could remove it. After that, my sweetheart would belong only to me: she would think only of me. As long as I was happy, the beautiful collar would remain gold; but if I fell into trouble the collar would turn red as blood. Then my sweetheart would say to her parents, "I am going to die. Bury me in a bridal dress, with a crown of orange-blossom on my head, and with a bunch of white roses at my girdle." She will fall asleep. All the world will believe her dead, they will bury her thus clothed, and she will lie sleeping, always sleeping, as long as my trouble remains with me. If I die, she will never wake. If my trouble leaves me, I will come and wake her, and we two will be married.'

'Apprentice, handsome apprentice, forge for me this collar of gold!'

'Little maiden, I will.'

In seven hours the beautiful collar that shone like the sun was ready. The lad tempered it in the burning coals; he took the collar out all hot, cut his arm and let his blood flow over it. He tempered the collar again in the burning coals. Whilst it was still warm he fastened it about the little maiden's neck. It became one with her flesh, so much so that no power in heaven or earth could ever remove it.

'Appentice, handsome apprentice, now I am your sweetheart! Now, by virtue of this gold collar I belong only to you, I shall think only of you!'

On the next morning the smith arrived at the castle.

'Good morning, master.'

'Good morning, apprentice. Now you have been working for two months. I have come to see if all is well, and to do the finer work that is beyond your skill.'

'Will you examine my work, master?'

The lad showed the smith all that he had made: the beautiful rings, the magnificent coronets and necklaces, the exquisite earrings, the girdles, the bracelets. . . . And the smith laughed.

'Apprentice, I have nothing more to teach you. You know more than I. Now you are free to set up for yourself. But you would do me a favour if you would stay yet three months more in my workshop.'

'Master, your will is mine. As long as you wish I will stay in your workshop.'

Then the smith and the lad went to find the marquis.

'Good morning, my lord marquis.'

'Good morning, my friends. What is it you wish?'

'My lord marquis, we have no more to do here. My apprentice has done the work even better than I myself could have done. It is he you must pay.'

'Apprentice, here are a thousand gold pieces.'

'My lord marquis, I thank you. I will take them for my mother.'

The smith and the lad left the castle. The lad went to his mother. 'Mother! Mother, you are poor no longer!' And he gave her the thousand gold pieces.

His mother wept for joy. 'Oh my son, the smith is not a bad man after all!'

'Time will show,' said the lad, and went back to the smith.

A week later the smith said, 'Apprentice, today we are going to the great fair in the next town. I have business there. We will drink a cup of wine together before we start.'

The lad took the cup of wine and drank. 'To your health, master!'

But the smith only pretended to drink. For he had put in the wine a drug so strong, so strong that at once the lad fell to the ground, sleeping like a log.

Then the smith bound the lad's hands and feet with strong chains; he gagged his mouth with thick linen. When the lad came to his senses, the forge was flaming like an inferno and the smith was brandishing a red-hot iron bar.

'Apprentice, rascally apprentice, you wished to know more than your master! Now you are in my power! None will come to deliver you. If you do not obey me you shall suffer sorrow and pain. Will you marry my daughter, the Queen of the Vipers?'

The lad could not speak because of the gag in his mouth. He shook his head.

The smith brought the red-hot iron bar close to the lad's feet and burned the soles of his shoes.

'Apprentice, rascally apprentice, will you marry my daughter, the Queen of the Vipers?'

The lad shook his head.

The smith held the red-hot bar close to the lad's face, and singed the hair on his forehead.

'Apprentice, rascally apprentice, for the third and last time, will you marry my daughter, the Queen of the Vipers?'

The lad shook his head.

Then the smith saw that he was wasting his time. He rushed out, harnessed his horse into a cart, picked up the lad, all bound and gagged, flung him into the cart, covered him with straw, and drove off at a furious gallop.

He drove, drove, drove. At sunset he came into a country of pines and mountains, on the borders of the great sea, the country ruled over by the Queen of the Vipers. In that country there was a high tower, without doors, without windows, without a roof, but with a well in the middle of the floor. The Queen of the Vipers alone could enter and leave that tower through a trap in the floor, which she opened and shut with a flick of her tail.

The smith drove to the foot of the tower, lifted the lad out of the cart, and laid him on the ground. He brought out of the cart also a heap of gold and of silver and of precious stones; he brought out a forge and all the necessary tools.

'Apprentice, rascally apprentice, who sought to know

more than your master,' said he, 'you are now my prisoner. I am about to call the Eagle of the Mountains to carry you inside this tower. And in this tower you will work for me in sorrow and pain until you consent to marry the Queen of the Vipers. All your work the eagle will bring me. You will drink the well water. And every day in exchange for your work, but only if the work be good, the eagle will bring you a scrap of bread, a scrap of bread black as the pit, and bitter as gall.'

Then the smith called the Eagle of the Mountains, and the great bird flew down. The smith took the chains from the lad's limbs and the gag from his mouth, and the Eagle of the Mountains lifted the lad, flew with him to the top of the tower, flew with him down inside the tower, and laid him on the bare ground beside the well. The eagle flew out of the tower and into the tower many times, bringing the gold, the silver, the precious stones, the forge, and all the necessary tools. And when he had brought all, the eagle flew off, leaving the lad alone.

The smith drove the empty cart back to his workshop. In the country of the Queen of the Vipers all was silent: and far, far away, in the castle of the marquis, the gold collar round the neck of the lad's little sweetheart turned red as blood.

'My father and my mother,' said the lad's little sweetheart, 'I feel I am going to die. When I am dead, bury me in a bridal robe, with a crown of orange-blossom on my head, and a bunch of white roses at my girdle.'

And after she had said that, the little sweetheart lay down on her bed, shut her eyes, and fell asleep. White as the winter snow, cold as the winter ice—there she lay, and all the world believed her dead. So they dressed her as she had bidden them, and laid her in the burial vault. For seven years she lay in that vault, sleeping, always sleeping.

And for seven years the lad lived and worked alone in the tower, with no bed but the bare ground, and no roof over him but the sky. If he thirsted, he drank the water from the well; and every day the Eagle of the Mountains brought him a scrap of bitter black bread, and carried away to the smith the work that he had finished.

But the lad did not work only for his master. Under his forge he had dug a deep hole, there to hide the things he was making for himself. First he made for himself an axe of fine steel, an axe large and well ground. Then he made for himself an iron belt, an iron belt furnished with three great hooks. Next he made for himself a pair of gold boots, gold boots reaching to his knees. And last he made for himself a pair of golden wings, wings light, light as a feather.

And every evening at sunset, the Queen of the Vipers came into the tower through the trap in the ground, the trap that she opened and shut with a flick of her tail.

'Apprentice, handsome apprentice, your martyrdom shall end as soon as you marry me.'

'Be gone, Queen of the Vipers! I have a sweetheart already. I will never forget her, never, never, never!'

So the lad said every evening.

But there came an evening when all was ready: the axe, the belt with its three iron hooks, the gold boots reaching to his knees, the golden wings—all were made and hidden in the hole under the forge.

That evening the Queen of the Vipers came in through her trap in the floor: 'Apprentice, handsome apprentice, why must you suffer? Marry me and your martyrdom will end.'

The lad stretched out his arms to the Queen of the Vipers: 'Come, come, my queen! The little sweetheart lies cold and still in the burial vault. Of what use to remember her?'

The Queen of the Vipers came to coil herself in the lad's arms. They embraced: they talked of love all through the night until the sun rose.

'Apprentice, handsome apprentice, your martyrdom is at an end. Soon I shall be your wife. Adieu! I will come again this evening. I will come at the setting of the sun. Then I will call the Eagle of the Mountains to lift you out of your prison.'

'Adieu, Queen of the Vipers. The time between now and
sunset will seem long to me!'

That evening an hour before sunset the lad said to himself,
'Now we are going to laugh!'

From the deep hole under his forge he took his sharp axe.
He buckled on his iron belt, his iron belt fitted with three
great hooks. He put on his high gold boots. Then he went to
stand against the wall, close to the trap in the ground, the trap
that the Queen of the Vipers opened every evening with a
flick of her tail.

At sunset the Queen of the Vipers came gliding through
the trap. The lad set his foot on her neck. She writhed and
hissed, but her fangs bit at the golden boot in vain. With one
blow of his axe the lad cut off her head. He hung her head onto
one of the hooks on his belt, and her body on another hook.
Then he put on his golden wings, his golden wings light as a
feather, and flew to the top of the tower.

Night came: the lad looked up at the sky to guide his way
by the stars. All at once he took flight, a hundred times more
swiftly than any swallow.

He flew, flew, till he came to his home village. There he
alighted on the church tower and looked down over the village to the smith's house and the meadow by the river. There
he listened, watched, and waited.

The church clock strikes eleven. The smith opens the door
of his house very softly, and looks all round him. He sees no
one: he hears nothing. He puts his hand to his mouth and calls
in the manner of a grasshopper: '*Cree! Cree! Cree!* Come my
daughter. Come, Queen of the Vipers! *Cree! Cree! Cree!*'

But the Queen of the Vipers does not come.

The smith waits and waits, he gets impatient, it is nearing
midnight. He hurries down to the meadow by the river bank,
takes off his clothes and his skin, turns into an otter, hides his
clothes and his skin in the hollow willow tree, and plunges
into the river. The lad opens his great golden wings, he flies
down a hundred times more swiftly than a swallow, and alights

beside the hollow willow tree. In less than no time the smith's skin is hanging from the third hook on the lad's iron belt. The lad rises once more on his golden wings and skims above the river.

'Ho! Smith! Ho, ho, ho!'

'What do you want with me, great bird?'

'Smith, I bring you news of your daughter, the Queen of the Vipers.'

'Speak, great bird!'

'Smith, I am no great bird. I am your apprentice. For seven years I have suffered pain and grief, shut in a tower in the country of pines and of mountains, on the borders of the great sea, the country ruled over by your daughter, the Queen of the Vipers. Smith, do you ask me for news of your daughter? Listen! Your daughter is in two pieces, the head and the body, and both the head and the body are hooked onto my iron belt. Catch! You are welcome to them! I fling them into the river. You are a master-welder. Try now if you can weld this head and body together again!'

Two great splashes! A terrible cry from the otter in the river. The voice of the lad speaking again:

'Smith, your sufferings are not yet ended. Search for your man's skin in the hollow willow tree. Search, search, my friend, but you will not find it. Your man's skin hangs from the third hook on my iron belt. And now you are an otter for ever and ever.'

Then the lad flew off, a hundred times more swiftly than any swallow, alighted at his mother's door, and furled his golden wings.

Knock! Knock!

'Who knocks?'

'Open, mother!'

'Heaven be praised! Is it you, my son? These seven years I have waited and waited!'

'Mother, blow up the ashes of the fire. Pile on dry wood. I have something here to burn.'

The mother blew up the ashes of the fire, and piled on dry wood. The fire blazed up. The lad took the smith's skin and flung it on the flames.

'Heaven preserve us, my son! You are burning the skin of a man!'

'No, mother, the skin of a demon. See how the flames devour it! See how it shrivels and turns to ashes. . . . And now, mother, I must leave you again. But soon I will come back to you, soon, very soon, and then you shall be blessed.'

Then the lad spread his golden wings once more, and took flight, a hundred times more swiftly than any swallow. In five minutes he stood at the door of the burial vault in the grounds of the marquis's castle. He took a lamp which burned there night and day; he went to the tomb where his little sweetheart lay sleeping. He lifted the lid of the tomb.

'Ho, little sweetheart, wake up! You have been sleeping for seven years.'

'Apprentice, handsome apprentice, you have come at last! You suffer no longer then? Apprentice, handsome apprentice, I have done all that you bade me do. See, I am wearing my bridal dress, and my crown of orange-blossom. See, the bunch of white roses is fastened in my belt.'

'Little sweetheart, stand up!'

The little sweetheart stood up. Hand in hand, she and the lad went out of the vault. Hand in hand, they came to the door of the marquis's castle.

'Little sweetheart, the household is still a-bed. Go softly, softly to your room, and do not come out until I call you.'

'Apprentice, handsome apprentice, I will obey you in all things.'

The little sweetheart tiptoed up to her room. The lad waited outside the castle until those in the house got up. Then he went in. The marquis and his lady sat at breakfast.

'Good morning, my lord! Good morning, my lady! Do you remember me?'

'No, my friend, we do not.'

'My lord and my lady, I am the smith's apprentice. Seven years ago I worked here for two months, making fine ornaments for your elder daughter, the bride of the King of the Isles.'

'True, true, apprentice; now we remember you!'

'My lord and my lady, you have a younger daughter.'

'Alas, alas, seven years ago we laid our younger daughter in the grave.'

'My lord and my lady, if I give you back your little daughter alive and well, will you swear that I shall marry her?'

'Oh gladly, how gladly!'

'My lord and my lady, send for the priest. As for me, I go to fetch your daughter.'

The lad went upstairs and called outside the little sweetheart's room. 'Come, little sweetheart, come!'

She opened her door, she took his hand. 'Apprentice, handsome apprentice, is it true that I shall marry you?'

'Yes, little sweetheart, it is true.'

What more to tell, but of joy, joy? The priest came, the lad fetched his mother, the little sweetheart and the lad were married. And they all lived happily ever after.

The Small Men and the Weaver

There are the Small Men, not a foot high, and they live under the earth and in the crevices of rocks. They have hoards of gold down there under the earth; and each year they carry up all their gold and spread it for one hour in the rays of the sun. Because, if they don't show their gold to the sun once a year, that gold turns red; and then the Small Men believe it to be poisonous and throw it away.

They keep flocks of tiny cows and sheep, too; and they grow corn and grapes and all manner of fruits. But their harvest is not like ours; they don't sow in spring and reap in autumn. All of their grain and fruit and vegetables grows and ripens at midnight on the last day of the year; and it must be gathered in and carried underground between that midnight and the following sunrise, otherwise it just vanishes.

That's all about the Small Men for the moment. And now about the weaver.

The weaver was out of work, poor, very poor, and he had a big family to feed. So it was his habit to go out at night into the fields to catch rabbits: some for his family to eat, and some for his wife and children to sell next day in the market.

So, on the last night of the year, the weaver said to his wife, 'You and the children go to bed. I'm off rabbiting.' And he took his ferret and his net and set out.

It was very cold that night, the ground was frozen, and the stars shone big and bright. The weaver went along, and he went along, till he came to a place of rocks and rabbit holes. He was just about to put his ferret into one of these holes, when he heard, among the rocks under his feet, a shrill voice calling out: 'Come along! Come along! None of your loitering there! The time is close on midnight! Hurry! Hurry! Hurry!'

And then there came the *click-clack, click-clack* of little sabots, and thousands of squeaky little voices piping up from among the rocks, 'We're coming, Master! We're coming!'

'Oh ho!' thinks the weaver. 'That must be the Small Men getting ready for their yearly harvest.' And he put the ferret back in his pocket, and stood quiet to watch.

First thing he saw was a little man with a whip in his hand leaping up out of a rabbit hole. The little man wasn't more than a foot high; he had long hair and a bushy beard, and he was wearing a shaggy bonnet, a red coat, and silver sabots. He came to perch on the top of a rock, looked up at the sky, cracked his whip, and called out, 'Midnight by the stars! Hurry, hurry, lazy-bones! Everything must be sown and reaped and got underground before sunrise!'

'Coming, Master, coming!'

And up from among the rocks sprang thousands of Small Men, with long hair and bushy beards, wearing shaggy bonnets, red coats, and silver sabots, just like the Master. The Small Men were carrying sickles, scythes, flails, pruning-hooks, baskets, sacks of corn and grass seed, iron bars to winnow corn, cattle goads and yokes: everything to sow and gather in the harvest, and lead in the cattle. Off they ran to begin their work, whilst the Master stood on his rock, cracked his whip, and screamed out, 'Hurry, hurry, hurry!'

And when the last of the Small Men had scampered past him, the Master tucked his whip under his arm, turned to the weaver and said, 'If you stand there gaping, mister weaver, you'll be frozen stiff presently. Would you like to earn half a crown?'

'I wouldn't mind,' said the weaver.

'Well then, stir yourself, stir yourself! Give a hand to my people!'

So the weaver followed after the Small Men, and found
them at work in tiny fields. They had already sown their seed,
the corn and the hay was already ripe, and now they were

cutting it. They were gathering grapes, too, in tiny vineyards,
and picking tiny pears and apples from tiny trees in tiny
orchards; and in tiny meadows they were rounding up cattle
no bigger than terriers, and sheep no bigger than weasels. And

all this they were doing in a place where, before that night, the weaver had never seen anything but a dry, desolate waste of grass and weeds.

All night, between midnight and sunrise, the Small Men worked at a run. They loaded the cut corn and hay into little carts no bigger than pumpkins, and the weaver piled a dozen of these little carts one on top of the other, and carried them to the place where the Master of the Little Men stood on his rock, cracking his whip and never ceasing to cry, 'Hurry, sluggards, hurry!' The weaver carried armfuls of little baskets, too, filled up with grapes and fruit; and he even carried armfuls of little sheep and cattle; and everything that he brought to the Master's rock, some of the Small Men dragged down the burrow and underground.

So, just before the sun rose, everything was gathered in, and the place where the fields and orchards had been, turned again into a barren waste of grass and withered weeds.

'Here's your half-crown, weaver,' said the Master, skipping off his rock. 'Would you like to earn another?'

'That I would!' said the weaver.

'Then stir yourself, stir yourself, give a hand to my people! There's no rest for them yet.'

And he jumped back onto his rock, began cracking his whip again, and calling out, 'Hurry, hurry, hurry! The sun is about to rise! Bring out the gold, you sluggards, that it may see its hour of daylight!'

Then up from every rabbit hole, and out from every crack in the rocks, the Small Men came again, staggering under tiny sacks of gold. They laid down the sacks at the weaver's feet, and the weaver shook out the gold in places where the rocks were smooth; and there it lay bright-glittering in the rays of the rising sun. And all the time the Master was cracking his whip and watching the sun and calling, 'Hurry, sluggards, the hour is passing, the hour is passing! . . . Gather up the gold again and bring it underground!'

The weaver and the Small Men worked at a run. The

weaver gathered up the gold again and stuffed it into the sacks, and the Small Men dragged the sacks once more underground.

'The hour is passed!' cried the Master, just as the last sack of the sun-touched gold had been carried down. 'Here is your second half-crown, weaver, and thank you for your help. But oh these lazy good-for-nothing men of mine! What sluggards they are, what sluggards! We have still three hundredweight of gold underground that hasn't seen the sun for a year. Now that three hundredweight has turned red, and is worthless, and all because my men wouldn't work faster!'

The weaver thought the Small Men had worked faster than he had ever seen anyone work in his life. But he put the half-crown in his pocket and only said 'Thank you'. He hadn't caught a single rabbit, but still he had earned five shillings, and that would buy his family bread for the day.

But what was the Master doing now? He was cracking his whip again and calling, 'Bring out the unclean gold, sluggards! Bring it out, bring it out, before it poisons our dwelling-place!'

Then out came the Small Men again, looking very tired, as well they might, and each one bent double under a tiny bulging sack. The Master jumped off his rock and led them to the waste place of grass and withered weeds. And there the Small Men set down and opened their sacks, and poured out the heaps of gold that shone red as fire in the bright sunlight.

And when the sacks were all emptied the Master cracked his whip and shouted 'All underground!' And in a twinkling the Small Men and the Master had gone.

And there was the weaver standing staring down at the heaps of red gold.

Three hundredweight, had the Master said? Yes, surely all of three hundredweight, and even more! Now the weaver worked faster than *he* had ever worked in his life, plucking up weeds and grass and anything he could lay hands on to cover that red gold. And when it was hidden, he put two of the red gold coins into his pocket and ran home.

'What, no rabbits?' says his wife.

'No, no rabbits,' says the weaver; 'but here's five shillings to buy bread.'

'Where did you get that?' says his wife.

'Tell you by and by,' says the weaver, and off he runs again, runs, runs, and never stops to draw breath till he gets to the town.

In the town he sought out a goldsmith and showed him the two pieces of red gold. 'Are these as good as yellow gold?' says he.

'Every bit,' says the goldsmith.

'Will you change them for small money?'

'Willingly,' says the goldsmith.

So the weaver got a pocketful of small money and went back home. He was so tired that he flopped into bed and slept for fifteen hours. When he woke up, he told his wife about the Small Men and everything.

Then the whole family, man, wife, and children, took sacks and went to the place where the weaver had hidden the red gold. They gathered it into the sacks and carried it home among them, the whole three hundredweight of it. And after that, the weaver bought a horse and cart, and they all moved out of their poor little house, and set off with their gold for another province. There the weaver, rich now as any lord, bought a fine manor with gardens and woods and twenty farms and a water-mill.

They were the richest folk in all the countryside. They lived happily. And they were always very good to the poor, remembering how poor they had once been themselves.

Tam and Tessa

Once upon a time there was a man whose wife had died, and left him with a little daughter called Tessa. And there was a woman whose husband had died, and left her with a little girl called Tam. So the man married the woman, and the little girls grew up together. These little girls were very pretty and so much alike they might have been twins; but Tam was vain and lazy, and Tessa was gentle and kind.

Now when the man and woman had been married for many years, and the little girls were big girls, and the lads came seeking them for sweethearts, Tam's mother said to Tessa's father, 'My Tam was seventeen yesterday. How old is Tessa?'

'Round about seventeen, I reckon,' said the man. 'I can't remember to a day. It makes no odds, does it?'

And the woman said, 'Yes, it makes a lot of odds. Here are all these lads come a-courting, and it's only right that the elder girl should be married first.'

So then the man said that Tessa must be the elder; and the woman said no, Tam must be the elder. And they talked and argued, talked and argued; but which of those two girls was the elder—no, they couldn't agree about that.

So the woman gave each of the girls a little fishing-net and a basket. 'Go down to the river and fish,' said she. 'And whichever of you brings back the most fish, that one shall be the elder of you.'

Tam and Tessa went down to the river to fish. Tessa tucked up her skirts and waded into the water. But Tam sat on the bank, sunning herself and thinking about the lads.

Tessa from *Tam and Tessa*

So Tessa said, 'Tam, Tam, why do you sit looking into the water? Come and fish!'

Tam said, 'Isn't the water cold?'

Tessa said, 'Yes, it is.'

Tam said, 'And aren't the stones on the river-bed scratching your feet?'

Tessa said, 'Yes, they are.'

'Well then, it's nicer on the bank.'

But then Tessa reminded Tam of what their mother had said. And Tam, who very much wanted to be the elder and get married first, took up her fishing-net and her basket and waded into the river.

'Oh, oh, oh! How cold it is! And oh my poor little feet!'

She caught four fish, but Tessa had already caught ten. So Tam said to Tessa, 'You're shivering and blue in the face. Go out on the bank and dry yourself in the sun.'

Tessa was really very cold. So she said, 'Well, for a few minutes then.' And she waded out onto the bank, set down her basket of fish on the edge of the water, wrapped herself in her shawl and—oh dear me, she fell asleep.

And what did Tam do but take all Tessa's fish and tip them into her own basket. Then she gave Tessa a shake. 'Wake up,' said she, 'I've got enough fish, I'm going home.' And off she walked.

Tessa went to pick up her basket. It was empty. 'You've taken my fish! You've taken my fish!' she cried.

And Tam called back over her shoulder, 'Why should I take your fish? I have already fourteen of my own. But whilst you slept the crows came down. No doubt it was they who took your fish.' And off she hurried to carry the fourteen fish to her mother.

Tessa went into the river again. She fished and fished. But she only caught three small fishes; and one of them was so tiny that she thought to throw it back into the water.

But the tiny fish spoke up and said, 'Little sister, take me with you!'

So Tessa went home with her three fishes. She gave two to her stepmother; but the very tiny one she kept, because it had called her sister. So she put it into a well, a little distance from the house, and fed it and made a pet of it.

Next day the stepmother said to Tessa, 'Tam is the elder of you, as I always thought. And I will see to it that she marries very soon. Now she must stay at home and make her bride's dress. Go you and pasture the goats.'

Tessa led the goats to pasture by the well. She sat down by the well to eat her dinner of rice. 'Teerock! Teerock!' she called. 'Little brother I have rice for you! Come and eat with your sister.'

And the little fish put his little nose up out of the well, and ate the rice that Tessa scattered for him.

So every day Tam sat at home stitching at her bride's dress, and Tessa led the goats to pasture. And every day she ate her dinner by the well, and shared her rice with the little fish Teerock. They loved each other very much, did Tessa and the little fish Teerock; it seemed they had only one heart between them. And Tessa laughed and said, 'Little brother Teerock, I am so happy! I am glad Tam stole my fish: if she hadn't stolen my fish I should never have known you, little brother.'

But Teerock answered, 'My sister, my sister, Tam does not love you. She will do us a mischief if she can. See, there she comes spying on you.'

Now it was true that Tam didn't like Tessa any more. First because she felt bad about having stolen Tessa's fish; and second because she wondered what made Tessa so happy. She thought Tessa ought to be jealous of her—*she* going to be married so soon, and making her bride's dress, whilst Tessa was only herding goats!

So Tam spied on Tessa, and came softly to the well, and heard her talking and laughing. Little fish Teerock went down to the bottom of the well and hid; but there were the grains of rice floating on the surface of the water.

Says Tam, 'To whom were you talking?'

Says Tessa, 'To anyone who cared to listen.'

Says Tam, 'Why have you scattered your rice on the water?'

Says Tessa, 'In case someone might be hungry.'

Says Tam, 'Who is that someone?'

Tessa wouldn't tell her. But Tam was determined to find out. And before sunrise next morning she went and hid by the well.

By and by Tessa came with the goats. She scattered some grains of rice on the surface of the water and called, 'Little brother Teerock! Little brother Teerock!'

And little brother Teerock came up to the surface and ate the rice; and he and Tessa talked and laughed together.

And whilst they were talking and laughing, and not heeding anything but their two selves, Tam slipped out of her hiding-place, and drove the goats away into a neighbouring farmer's cornfield.

The goats were leaping and skipping and playing havoc with that cornfield: the farmer saw them and he was angry. He drove the goats out of the field and locked them up in a barn.

So by and by Tessa stopped talking to her little brother fish and looked round. No goats! Up she jumped and ran about for a long time looking for them. She was looking for them all day; and when it came evening she met a lad and asked if he had seen her goats.

'Yes,' said the lad, 'they were making havoc in master's cornfield, and he's taken them and locked them up in his barn.'

So away went Tessa to the farmer to get back her goats; and by the time she had driven them home it was quite late.

And what was Tam doing? Tam had gone back to the well. She leaned over it and whispered in a sweet little voice, as like to Tessa's voice as she could make it, 'Little brother Teerock! Little brother Teerock!'

The little fish came to the surface of the water. In an instant Tam had caught him between her two hands. Ah ha, little brother Teerock! You may flap and wriggle as much as you like! Tam has you, and she isn't going to let you go!

Tam carried the little fish home and killed him. She cut him into three slices, dipped the slices in vinegar and broiled them. She gobbled up two slices, but then she got such a pain that she couldn't eat any more, so she left the third slice in a dish on the shelf.

When Tessa had driven the goats home she went back to the well. 'Little brother Teerock!' she called. 'I've come to tell you I've found the goats, and I've brought some more rice for you.' She scattered the rice on the water: but no little fish rose up to eat it. 'Little brother Teerock, are you asleep down there? Well then, goodnight! I'll see you in the morning.'

But in the morning, when she drove the goats to pasture by the well, and scattered rice on the water, and called, no little fish put up his snout to nibble the rice. She called, called, called. She spent hours calling. No little fish! So at last she gave up calling, and began to sob.

'Someone has stolen my little brother,' she sobbed. 'Now I have no friend in all the world!'

And she gathered the goats together and went home weeping.

That night she had a dream. She dreamed that she was still sobbing and that little fish Teerock came to her and said, 'Little sister, dry your tears. My little sister loved little fish Teerock very dearly. But Tam came and killed him. She cut him into three slices and broiled him. Two slices she ate, but then little fish Teerock gave her such a pain that she couldn't eat the last slice of him, and she put that last slice in a dish on a shelf. Go, little sister, take that last slice, put it in a coconut and hide it under the grass at the cross-roads. Do not drive the goats to pasture by the well any more, but drive them onto the common beyond the cross-roads. So that both on going out and on coming home, you may pass the place where the last slice of me lies hidden.'

Next morning Tessa did what little fish Teerock had told her in her dream. She found that last slice of him, put it in a coconut, wrapped the coconut in her apron, and drove the goats towards the common beyond the cross-roads. At the cross-roads she hid the coconut under some long grass; and every day, as she passed and repassed the place where the coconut lay hidden, she lifted the long grass from over it and said, 'Little brother Teerock, do you still love me?'

And a voice answered out of the coconut, 'Yes, sister Tessa, I love you always.'

But one day when she came to lift the grass from the coconut, the coconut was gone. And in its place she found a pair of golden sandals. And the sandals said, 'Take us home, sister Tessa.'

And then, just as Tessa stooped to pick up the sandals, a big black crow flew down, seized one of those golden sandals in his beak and flew away with it. Oh how Tessa cried! But what could she do? She could only pick up the other sandal, hide it under her apron, and carry it home.

The crow flew and flew, he came to the young king's palace, and there he dropped the golden sandal at the gate of the palace. The young king saw it and said, 'This is the sign I have been waiting for! Whomsoever this sandal fits, her I will marry.'

Well, well, all the girls from a hundred miles round came to try on that sandal; but it wouldn't fit any of them. If the girl's foot was small, it made itself big; if the girl's foot was big, it made itself small. The courtiers said, 'The very devil is in this sandal!' And the young king said, 'It seems that I am not meant to marry after all!'

So when Tam heard about the sandal, she flung down the bride's dress she was making. 'I'm off to the palace,' said she. 'For why should I be the bride of a country lad if I can marry a king?'

And Tessa's father said to Tam's mother, 'If your Tam goes, my Tessa must go too!' The mother wasn't willing, but Tessa's father got angry and shouted. So Tessa wrapped up the pair to the sandal in her apron and followed Tam to the palace.

When Tam tried on the sandal she gave a shriek, for if it

had been a crab it couldn't have pinched her more fiercely. But when Tessa tried it on, it fitted her to perfection. And Tessa took the other sandal out from under her apron, and said, 'Here is the pair to it.'

'Where did you get it?' cried the young king, all in a maze.

Tessa said, 'I found it at the cross-roads.'

And the young king said, 'Then you are my bride, lovely Tessa!' And he married her that very day.

Tam went home raging with jealousy. She stormed and wept. 'I'll kill that Tessa, I will, I will!' she screamed.

The father said, 'Hold your noise.' But the mother whispered in Tam's ear, 'Have patience, I'll see you righted!'

So when Tessa had been married for several months, and was happy as happy (she loving the young king with all her heart, and he loving her just as well), Tessa's father had to go on a journey to a neighbouring town to sell some of his goats, and to hire a goatherd to look after those he kept, for Tam wouldn't herd them, no, not she! Herding goats had never been *her* work, she said.

So Tessa's father set out, and Tam's mother whispered, 'Now is our chance!' And she hurried off to the palace to see the king.

'Oh sire,' said she, 'today we are moving house; my man is away and we have no one to help us pack up. Will you lend us my dear little daughter Tessa just till tomorrow?'

The young king wasn't willing, but Tessa said, 'I think I ought to go.' So then the king said very well, but she must come back tomorrow morning without fail.

'Without fail, sire,' said Tam's mother, curtsying low.

Then Tessa went off with her stepmother, and when she came to their home, Tam up and hit her across the face, and cried out, 'Ho, my lady queen, none of your fine airs here!' And they kept her hard at work all day, though they weren't moving house at all. They gave her nothing to eat, and when night came they made her sleep on the floor.

In the morning, when Tessa thought to go back to the palace, the stepmother said, 'You shall go soon. But the olives are ripe and I'm busy. You and Tam must go and pick them.'

And she gave Tam and Tessa each a basket, and sent them out to pick the olives. But into Tam's basket she put a great axe and whispered, 'Do what you will with it, but do it secretly.'

So when they got among the olive trees, Tam said to Tessa, 'You are lighter than I am. You climb up and pick the olives, and I'll stand underneath with my basket and catch them as you throw them down.'

And Tessa climbed up into the tree.

But no sooner was she up, than Tam began hacking at the tree with her great axe.

'Sister, sister,' cried Tessa, 'what are you doing?'

'Pride goes before a fall,' says Tam, chopping away with the axe.

So then Tessa knew that Tam meant to kill her, and she daren't come down. But as the trees grew close together she swung herself from the one she was on into the next one.

And *chop, chop, chop,* went Tam at this second tree with her great axe.

Tessa swung herself into a third tree, into a fourth, into a fifth: but always there was Tam down below, chopping away, until Tessa had come to the last tree of all, and that was a little tree on the very edge of the river. And there was Tam standing underneath this little tree, and chop, chop, chopping with her great axe.

'Sister, sister,' cried Tessa, 'what have I done that you should treat me so?'

But Tam only grinned and said again, 'Pride goes before a fall, my lady queen!' And chopping away with all her strength, she made such a gaping wound in the trunk of that little tree that it toppled over and fell into the river,

And Tessa fell with it.

So then Tam went home and told the stepmother that Tessa had fallen into the river and been drowned.

But Tessa hadn't been drowned. She had turned into a golden turtle. And the golden turtle swam away down the river.

That same day the stepmother went with Tam to the palace, and asked to see the king.

'Where is Queen Tessa?' said the king.

'Oh sire!' cried the stepmother. 'She fled away from us in the night. We have sought her and sought her, but not a trace of her have we found. Now I have brought you my daughter to take her place.'

'*Take her place!*' shouted the king. 'Are you mad?' And he called his guards and bade them put both mother and daughter in prison. But the mother wept and begged for grace, that she might go and search for Tessa. She would leave her own daughter as a hostage, she said; and if Tessa couldn't be found—well then, let the king kill them both. So the king relented, for he had a kind heart. Tam stayed at the palace, and the stepmother went home well content. 'For Tam is every whit as beautiful as Tessa,' she said to herself. 'And in time, when Tessa is not found, why then, the king will comfort himself with Tam.'

But the young king didn't comfort himself with anybody or anything. He was sad, oh sad! He wept and moped. So one day his courtiers, hoping to divert him, arranged a hunt, to catch birds and fishes. The king didn't want to go, but they begged and prayed him, and at last he said, 'Oh, very well.' And off they set.

They rode through the forest and shot many birds; then they came down into a plain near the river. In the plain, not far from the river was a pool, brightly shining; and when they came near the pool, the king drew his hand across his eyes and said, 'Why does that pool so shine? Why does it make me think of my dear wife? Am I awake, or am I dreaming? Go, some of you, to the pool, and tell me why it shines.'

The courtiers left the king and went to the pool; and as they went they said to one another, 'Can our young king be going mad with grief?'

'And indeed am I going mad?' thought the poor young king, as he sat on his horse and waited.

By and by the courtiers came back. One of them was carrying a great golden turtle. 'Sire, it was the shining of this turtle that lit up the pool.'

'We will take it home,' said the king.

The king had a golden basin made for the golden turtle; and every day he went to feed it. He spent long hours beside the golden basin; he still felt very sad, but the sight of the turtle lightened his heart a little; though why it lightened his heart, he could not tell.

Meanwhile the stepmother pretended to be searching for Tessa, and Tam lived on at the palace. She was always at the king's elbow, flaunting herself, trying to attract him. 'Why won't you look at me?' she said. 'Am I not beautiful?'

'Yes, I suppose you are beautiful,' said the king. 'But I wish to be alone.' And he left her, and went away to sit by the golden basin and watch the turtle.

And Tam muttered to herself, 'I could kill that turtle! I *will* kill that turtle!'

And so, very early one morning, before the king was out of bed, she took the golden turtle from its golden basin, killed it, cooked it, and ate it.

When the king saw that the turtle was gone from the basin, he rushed about like a mad thing. 'Where is my turtle? Someone has taken it!'

'Well *I* didn't take it,' says that lying Tam. 'Why should I?'

But then the king said he would send for a diviner to find out the thief. And that threat so frightened Tam that she confessed.

The king said, 'I have deer, I have goats, I have sheep. Why, if you wanted meat, did you not eat one of these?'

'I felt ill,' says Tam. 'I had a longing for turtle flesh.'

'Get out of my sight!' cried the king. And he walked away and left her.

Now Tam had thrown the turtle shell outside in the courtyard. And out of that turtle shell there came a blackbird. The blackbird flew to the king's window and sang and sang. Its song was so wonderful that all the courtiers gathered under the window to listen. The song melted the king's heart with love and sorrow. He spoke to the blackbird, and it came to perch on his finger. The king had a golden cage made for the blackbird, to go into or come out from as it willed. The blackbird sang and sang. The king spent hours listening to that song.

But one day, when the king was busy with his ministers, and the blackbird sat silent in its cage, Tam came by. Oh wicked, wicked Tam! What did she do? She snatched the blackbird from its cage, she killed it and cooked it and ate it.

The king came back into his room. No blackbird! 'Where, oh where is my blackbird?' he cried.

'Well,' says Tam, 'I was cooking dinner. The blackbird came and fell into a pan of boiling water. So then it was dead and I ate it.'

The king said never a word. He was too sad to speak.

Tam threw the blackbird's feathers into the garden; and they turned into bamboo shoots. The king saw the bamboos. 'Strange!' said he. 'There were never bamboos here before!' And he sat a long time by the bamboo shoots, with his head in his hands, thinking.

So then, when the king had gone in to dinner, Tam cut the bamboo shoots and cooked them and ate them.

The king comes back into the garden. 'Where are my bamboo shoots?'

'Oh,' says Tam, 'I cooked them and ate them. I didn't know you wanted to keep them.'

'Go home to your mother,' cried the king. 'I can't bear to look on you!'

So Tam went home to her mother. But, before she went, she gathered up the husks of the bamboo shoots, carried them with her, and threw them away on the side of the high road, many miles from the palace.

And from those husks there grew up a pear tree. Its branches whispered in the wind and gleamed in the sun, and cast a refreshing shade over the dust of the high road.

Now there was an old woman who sold weaving combs, and as she was trudging home from market, she sat her down to rest under the shade of the pear tree. She looked up into the tree and saw one pear, high, high up; a pear round, ripe, beautiful. The dust of the high road had made the old woman's throat dry: she longed, longed for that pear. But it was high above her reach.

'Oh pear, beautiful pear,' says she, 'have pity on a thirsty old woman and fall into her basket!'

And the pear fell into her basket.

The old woman took the pear between her hands and looked at it. Thinks she, 'I may be thirsty, but this pear is too beautiful to eat.' And she took the pear home to her little tumbledown house, and put it in a jar full of rice. Then she drank some water, munched a crust of dry bread, filled up her basket with weaving combs and off with her to market again.

She didn't get home till evening. And then—oh my, oh my! What a surprise! She found the house swept, everything put tidy, the table spread, and supper all ready for her!

'This is more than strange!' thinks the old woman. 'I am poor, I have no relations, no good friends! Who can have done all this?' And she went to bed, mighty puzzled, but blessing the one who had so served her.

In the morning she is off to market again. And no sooner has she shut the door behind her, than the pear lifts itself out of the jar of rice. The pear shakes itself free of its skin. What comes from inside that skin? A beautiful young woman. Queen Tessa!

And Queen Tessa busies herself tidying up the old woman's little ruin of a house. 'But there are only two cracked plates,' says she; 'there is only one chipped cup. I must have plates, I must have cups, I must have a little tray to put the cups and plates on, I must have a little shelf where the tray may rest.' She snaps her fingers: there are the plates, there are the cups, there is the little tray, there is the shelf. And when the old woman came home that evening there was such a supper waiting for her as she had never had before in all her life.

'By men and by gods,' cries the old woman, 'who can have done all this?'

Next morning, the old woman took her basketful of weaving combs, went out, locked the door behind her, and stumped off as if she were going to market. But she hadn't gone far when she turned, came back to the house, crept in through a cellar window, and stole quietly, quietly upstairs and hid behind the kitchen door. She put her eye to the keyhole of the door and saw a young woman, beautiful as a fairy, sweeping up the dust from the kitchen floor.

The old woman watched and wondered: by and by the young woman put down the broom, took a jar and went out to fetch water from the spring. The old woman hopped into the kitchen, looked here, looked there. She peered into the rice jar—no pear, only the skin. The old woman took the skin, put it in her pocket, and went to hide behind the kitchen door again.

Back comes Queen Tessa with the water jar. She fills a pan with water and sets it on the fire. The old woman creeps up behind her and clears her throat, '*Ahem! Ahem!*'

Queen Tessa darts towards the rice jar. The pear skin has gone! She is discovered. She turns round and smiles at the old woman.

'Oh me! Oh me!' cries the old woman. 'Who are you, and where have you come from?'

So then Queen Tessa makes the old woman sit down, sits down herself, takes the old woman's hand, and tells her the whole story.

'And now,' says Queen Tessa, when the story is told, 'go to the palace. Ask to see the king and tell him that today you hold a great festival. Invite him to come to your house.'

'What, what—invite the *king* to come to my poor little ruin! How can I?'

But Queen Tessa said, 'Go, go. I will see to everything. Only don't say I am here.'

The old woman wasn't very willing; but she went. She found the king moping in the garden of the palace, and she knelt at his feet.

Says the king, 'Well, old woman, what can I do for you?'

Says the old woman, 'Your Majesty, today I hold a great festival. I am come to invite you to my house.'

The king looked at the old woman and made no answer. He thought she was mad.

So the old woman got up and made to go; and she was so bewildered and bothered that she began to cry.

So then the king called her back. 'Well, old woman, I will come if you will spread a velvet carpet from the palace to your house.'

So the old woman goes home. Heaven have mercy on us— what does she see? No poor little ruin, but a noble house with

gilded pillars and rows of glittering windows, and a great
garden in front of it; and in the garden a silk pavilion shining
with all the colours of the rainbow.

The old woman goes into the house. What does she see
now? A great marble hall with gold tables from end to end
of it, and the tables spread with every manner of food and
drink in gold dishes and silver vessels. And there is Queen
Tessa, robed like the queen she is, standing by the tables.

'Well,' says Queen Tessa, 'how do you like your house?
Are the meats and drinks of the best, and is there plenty of
them?'

'Oh!. . .Ah!. . .Oh!. . .' The old woman can scarcely
speak. 'But—but the king won't come unless there is a velvet
carpet laid all the way from here to the palace.'

'The king shall have his carpet. Go back and tell him so.
But speak no word of me.'

So the old woman sets out once more for the palace, and—
look, would you believe it?—as she goes along the streets a
velvet carpet unrolls itself behind her.

The king is still moping in the garden. The old woman
kneels at his feet and says, 'Your Majesty, the carpet is laid.'

The king went to the palace gates. He looked out. Marvel
of marvels! There is the velvet carpet stretching right through
the town to his very feet.

'I will come, old woman, I will come after sunset, when the
day is cooler.'

The old woman hurries home again. She is so scared and so
out of breath that she can hardly blurt out her news. But
Queen Tessa says, 'There is no need to be scared, old woman.
You have only to do exactly as I tell you.'

And they waited till sunset. Then came a great procession:
drummers and trumpeters marching in front, lords and ladies
following, the king in a litter born upon the shoulders of the
royal guards, and thousands of townsfolk bringing up the rear.

The old woman stood at the gate of her grand house. She
had Queen Tessa's orders, and she carried them out: the lords

and the ladies she bade go into the hall and seat themselves at the tables; the drummers and trumpeters she sent to be feasted in the great kitchens; the townsfolk were told to amuse themselves in the gardens, where refreshments would presently be served to them. But the king, with one or two of his ministers, she invited to step into the rainbow pavilion, where she would serve him with a special little collation before the feast.

So the king went into the pavilion and sat himself down. He was not happy, he was thinking always of his dear lost wife. All these magnificent preparations meant nothing to him: but there, he saw the old woman was trying hard to please him, and he behaved with courtesy as a king should.

The old woman brought him drink in a crystal goblet. The king put the goblet to his lips and tasted. Then he started up with a great cry: 'Old woman, old woman, who mixed this drink that is in my cup?'

'I mixed it myself, Your Majesty, does it not please you?'

'Not please me!' cried the king. '*Not please me!* It is the drink of all others that I like best! But no one knew how to mix it except my dear lost wife. Oh my queen, my queen, who taught this old woman the secret of your mixing?'

Then the old woman brought the king some little cakes laid out on a crystal dish. The king looked at the cakes, and the tears ran down his cheeks. He tasted one of the cakes, and again he started up. 'Old woman, old woman, who made these cakes?'

'A neighbour of mine, Your Majesty, who has come in to help me.'

'Old woman, you lie! There is no one on earth who can make such cakes except my dear lost wife. Old woman, where is my wife? Old woman have mercy, and tell me where she is?'

'I am here, my king.'

A curtain at the back of the pavilion is drawn aside. There stands Tessa!

'Oh my queen, my queen, my queen!' The king has her in his arms: the tears are still running down his cheeks, but they are tears of joy. No, he cannot eat, he cannot drink! Let others feast, but he and Queen Tessa must go back to the palace; for though he holds her in his arms, he can scarcely believe that she will not vanish again.

So he and Queen Tessa were carried in the litter back through the carpeted streets to the palace. And there Tessa, still with the king's arms holding her tight, told her whole story. And when the story was ended, the king cried out, 'Guards, let a great fire be lit in the courtyard! Bring hither the queen's stepmother and her daughter, and burn them to death!'

But Queen Tessa said, 'My king, now we are so happy, shall we not also be merciful?'

So the king said the guards needn't light the great fire. But he bade them drive Tam and her mother out of his kingdom.

Tessa's father he sent for, and having rated him soundly for not looking after Tessa more carefully, forgave him, and packed him off home again with a bag full of gold pieces. As for the old woman, she lived on in the fine house that had once been a poor little ruin, and the king gave her horses and carriages, money in plenty, and servants to wait on her.

Well, well, well—was there ever such an astonished and such a happy old woman as that old woman in all the world?

The Snake Monster

The Snake Monster

Once upon a time, on the top of a rock, high on a great mountain, there lived a monster snake. The snake's body was six hundred feet long, and thicker round than the trunk of the biggest oak that ever grew; he had eyes red as fire, and a tongue more sharp than any sword. He was so greedy that nothing could satisfy his appetite. Night and day he kept his great mouth open; and by his breath, flocks and herds, men and women, all living things were lifted from the earth like feathers, and plunged into his jaws. What was to be done? The land about the foot of the mountain was rich and fertile;

but no one dared to walk or to graze flocks within ten miles
of that mountain.

So, at last, the lord of the land sent drummers through all
the villages round about: *Dub-a-dub-dub! Dub-a-dub-dub!*
'Whosoever kills the snake monster shall be given a hundred
cows with their calves, a hundred mares with their foals, five
hundred sheep, and five hundred goats; and for all these
flocks and herds he shall have free grazing, all his life long, on
ten miles of pasture-land around the foot of the mountain.'

All very fine of my lord to make such a promise! But who
could get near the monster to kill him? Who indeed? Since to
draw near him was to be sucked up by his breath and swallowed.

Now there was a young blacksmith living in a village just
outside the range of the monster's breath. And one day this
young blacksmith said, 'Blacksmithing is a pleasant enough
trade; but to be master of all those promised flocks and herds,
and to exchange the heat and smoke of the forge for the
sweet air of the pasture-land—ah, that would be pleasanter
still! Yes, it is *I* who will kill that snake monster!'

The people in the young blacksmith's village said, 'It can't
be done!' The young blacksmith said, 'Yes, it can!' So what
did he do? He set to work and began tunnelling under the
ground outside his forge.

The village people, peeping into the tunnel, said, 'What's
the good of this?' The young blacksmith said, 'You wait and
see!' And the people shook their heads and said, 'Poor lad,
he's taken leave of his wits!'

But the young blacksmith went on tunnelling. He tunnelled and he tunnelled in the direction of the snake monster's
mountain; and though it took him a long, long time, at last
he had made a tunnel all the way from his forge to the foot of
the mountain. Then, at the mountain end of this tunnel, he
hollowed out an underground cave, with just a very small
opening to the outside world at the foot of the mountain.
And in this cave he set up a forge; and brought there, too, his

anvil, his bellows, his hammer, his tongs, a long iron chain, and great bars of iron as big round as his thigh.

In that tunnel, and in that cave, being underground, the young blacksmith was safe from the snake monster's breath. So forth and back, forth and back along that tunnel he trudged for many a weary day, bringing iron bars and more iron bars, till the cave was packed full of them.

And then what did he do? He drove an iron spike deep into the rock wall of the cave, and to this spike he fastened one end of his long iron chain. And the other end of the chain he fastened with a padlock about his waist.

'And now, snake monster,' says he, 'we will set to work and cook you a dinner!'

So he lit a fire on his forge and worked away with the bellows; and when the sparks flew and the fire blazed, he plunged into it, one after the other, seven of the great iron bars. And as each bar glowed red, he caught it up with his big tongs, and cast it outside the cave. And each bar, as he cast it out, was drawn up like a feather into the snake monster's mouth and swallowed. But the young blacksmith himself was not drawn up, because he was held fast by his iron chain to the rock of the cave. So back with him to his forge, to work the bellows, and heat seven more iron bars red-hot, and to cast them out, and see them lifted like feathers, up and up, to the top of the mountain, to be plunged into the snake monster's jaws.

'Are you feeling warm up there, old fellow?' laughed the blacksmith.

The snake monster *was* feeling warm. There was snow up there on the mountain-top, and the snake monster was taking great gulps of it to cool the heat that raged in his stomach. But scarcely was he feeling comfortable again, when up came another set of red-hot bars, and down they went into his tormented stomach. Why didn't the silly creature shut his mouth, one might well ask. Well, he couldn't; he never had shut his mouth in all his life, and now it was fixed open.

Day and night, day and night, for seven years the young blacksmith went on heating those iron bars, sleeping on his feet whilst the sparks flew round him, and eating and drinking whilst one hand worked the bellows, staggering out with one red-hot bar after another, seeing those bars soar up and up above his head to the top of the mountain, feeling the hair rise from his head with the snake monster's breath, but held securely on his feet by the strength of the chain about his waist.

And the snake monster, raging with thirst, was swallowing snow by the cart-load, and drying up all the streams that flowed down the mountain. But at last, at last, after seven years, there came a day when the heat inside him was so great that he burst with a noise like thunder: and that was the end of him.

The young blacksmith unfastened the chain from round his waist, and went back through the tunnel to his home. What a welcome awaited him! The people, who had heard the thunder of the monster's bursting, were gathered in their hundreds round his little house. They carried him in procession to the lord of the land, and the lord of the land gave him the promised reward: the hundred cows with their calves, the hundred mares with their foals, the five hundred sheep, and the five hundred goats, together with free grazing for all these flocks and herds on ten miles of rich pasture-land round the foot of the mountain.

Who so merry now as our young blacksmith? Who so jubilant as the grateful people? After many days, when all that was left of the snake monster was his bleached bones, the people climbed up the mountain and brought away those bones.

With those bones they built a church in the blacksmith's village. And a very fine church it was, all white and glistening.

The Young Shepherd

Once upon a time there was a spoilt little princess. And on a day in spring, when this little princess was walking in the fields with the king and queen, she saw a flock of sheep with their lambs skipping about them.

Oh, now the little princess wants a lamb, and what she wants she must have. So the king sends for the farmer and buys a lamb, and the princess ties her blue sash round the lamb's neck and leads it home in triumph.

All very well: but next morning the princess insists on leading the lamb into the fields herself, and she insists, too, on sitting in the fields with that lamb all through the day, and on leading it home again in the evening. And she does this every day till summer comes; and the sun blazes down on her, and the king and queen get vexed. The little princess has a delicate skin: now she is coming out in freckles; it won't do, she is ruining her complexion. Besides—who ever heard of a princess keeping sheep?

But the little princess will do as she will do. And if they wanted her to do otherwise—well then, they shouldn't have spoilt her.

By and by the lamb grew into a sheep; and by and by that sheep had a lamb. The little princess was in ecstasies. And when next year *that* lamb became a sheep and had twins—who more delighted than the princess? 'Very soon I shall own a great big flock of sheep,' said the little princess. 'And I shall shear them myself and sell the wool.'

So year by year, as the princess grew older, her flock of sheep increased, and she spent all her time in the fields tending the flock. She neglected her lessons; her beautiful dresses were all stained green with the grass; and as to freckles—well, her face was just yellow with them.

'It won't do!' said the queen in tears.

'No, it certainly will *not* do!' said the king. 'I must put my foot down!' And he stamped his foot to show that he really meant what he was saying. 'This very day I am going to find a shepherd to look after the princess's flock.'

So the king bustled out, and by and by he met a young lad with a fresh, merry face and a sprightly way with him.

Said the king to the lad, 'Good day, merry friend, and where might you be going?'

Said the lad to the king, 'To look for a master.'

Said the king, 'Shall I be your master?'

Said the lad, 'That depends on the wages.'

So the king offered big wages, and the lad agreed to shepherd the princess's flock.

The king went to the princess and said, 'I have found a shepherd for your flock.'

'But I don't want a shepherd!' said the princess.

'Wait till you see him,' said the king.

'Let him come here,' said the princess.

So the lad came laughing.

'What are you laughing at?' said the princess.

'At you, because you are so pretty,' said the lad. 'And

because I am to be your shepherd, and that pleases me.'

And the spoilt young princess said, 'Very well, you shall be my shepherd.' For there was something about the lad that won her heart.

'There will be no need for you to go to the fields any more,' said the queen.

The princess tossed her head and said, 'I must keep an eye on my shepherd. I shall go to the fields every morning and every evening, to lead out my sheep and to bring them home.'

'Well, well,' said the queen. 'In the early morning and in the evening the air is cool and won't spoil your complexion. And that at least is something to be thankful for!'

So every morning the princess set out with the shepherd to the fields, and showed him where he must graze her flock. And every evening she came to fetch her flock home again. Every day the king gave the shepherd a bottle of wine and a good supply of food; and every week he paid him a handsome wage. It was a fine easy life that young shepherd lived; and though he laughed at the princess and teased her—well, she seemed to like it.

One morning the princess led her flock to a big beautiful meadow; and on the borders of the meadow were three little woods, one to the north, one to the east, and one to the west.

'And whatever you do,' said the princess, 'don't you go into those three woods, for a giant lives in each of them. Now, you hear what I say?'

'Yes, I hear what you say,' answered the young shepherd.

But no sooner had the princess left him and gone back to the palace than what did that young shepherd do? He left the flock grazing peacefully, and away with him into one of the woods.

The young shepherd had a knife in his pocket, and in the handle of the knife was a whistle. So there he was, strolling through the wood and playing merry tunes on the whistle. And he hadn't gone far when he felt the ground under his feet tremble, and through the wood a giant came striding, a giant all dressed in steel.

Says the giant, 'Little rascal, what are you doing in my wood?'

Says the lad, 'Oh, just taking a walk. No harm in that, I suppose?'

'I don't know,' says the giant; and he began walking round the lad, staring down at him in a stupid kind of way.

Says he, 'What's that thing hanging on your back?'

'That's what they call a game-bag,' says the lad. 'I've got meat and bread in it, and a bottle of wine. Would you like some?'

'Yes, I would,' says the giant.

So the giant sat down, and the young shepherd sat down, and the young shepherd took the bread and meat and the bottle of wine out of his game-bag. But the giant was so greedy, that the young shepherd didn't get a mouthful to eat or a drop to drink; the giant gobbled up everything and drank down the wine at one gulp; and then he felt sleepy because he wasn't used to wine, and he lay down on his back and snored.

'All right,' said the young shepherd, 'that's the last meal you'll get, old fellow!'

And he cut off the giant's head with his knife.

Then he went on through the wood and came to a castle made of steel. Everything inside the castle was made of steel, tables, chairs, beds, cupboards—all steel. And there was a steel stable. And what should he see in the stable but a steel horse.

And when he had looked well at all these things, the young shepherd came out of the wood and went back into the meadow where the princess's flock was grazing.

In the evening comes the princess to drive her flock home.

'Have you been in the woods?' says she.

'No, I haven't been in the woods,' says the young shepherd. And that wasn't a lie, either, because he'd only been into one of them.

'Ah, how hot it's been today,' says he to the princess, as

they drove the flock back to the palace together. 'And how thirsty I am! All the wine in my bottle was emptied at one gulp.'

'Well then,' says the princess, 'tomorrow you shall have two bottles of wine. My father will give you one, and I will give you another. Only don't you tell him!'

So the next morning, before they set out with the flock, the

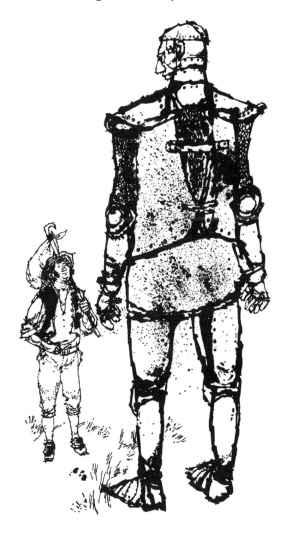

princess came to the young shepherd with a bottle of wine.
'But if you tell, I shall hate you!' said she.

'*I'm* not going to tell!' said the young shepherd.

The princess led her flock to the same meadow as yesterday.

'Now don't you go into the woods, mind!' said she to the
young shepherd.

'No, I won't go into the woods,' said he.

But no sooner had the princess left him, than away with
him into the second wood, strolling about in there and playing
merry tunes on his whistle. And it wasn't long before he felt
the ground tremble under his feet, and through the wood a
giant came striding, a giant all dressed in silver.

'Little rascal, what are you doing in my wood?'

'Oh, just taking a walk. No harm in that, I suppose?'

'Don't know,' says the giant. And he begins walking round
the lad, staring down at him in a stupid kind of way.

'What's that on your back?'

'A game-bag, with meat, bread, and two bottles of wine in
it. Would you like a taste?'

Of course the giant would like a taste! He ate all the bread,
he ate all the meat, he drank all the wine in two gulps. And the
wine made him sleepy, because giants aren't used to wine. So
he lay down on his back and snored.

And the young shepherd cut off the giant's head with his
knife.

Then he went on through the wood and came to a silver
castle: everything silver inside—beds, tables, chairs, curtains.
And there was a silver stable, with a silver horse in it.

And when the young shepherd had looked well at all these
things, he went back to the meadow where the sheep were
grazing.

In the evening comes the princess.

'Shepherd boy, have you been in the woods?'

'No, I haven't.'

'That's all right then. I've been worried. But what's the
matter?'

'I'm thirsty. It's been so hot!'

'Well then, tomorrow you shall have three bottles of wine: one the king will give you, and two I will give you. But don't you tell, or I shall hate you!'

'*I* won't tell.'

So next morning the young shepherd got his three bottles of wine, and he and the princess led out the sheep and took them to the same meadow. And again the princess told him not to go into the woods, and he said of course he wouldn't. But as soon as she left him—away with him into the third wood. And there he met a giant all dressed in gold, and the giant ate all the young shepherd's bread and meat, and drank down three bottles full of wine in three gulps, and fell asleep.

And the young shepherd served that giant just as he had served the other two, and went on through the wood and came to a castle built of gold, with everything gold in it, and a gold stable with a gold horse. And when he had looked well at all these things, he went back to the sheep in the meadow.

In the evening the princess comes to fetch him.

'Have you been in the woods?'

'No, I haven't been in the woods.'

'That's all right then. We'll go home.'

Now the princess was growing up, and the king and queen thought it was high time she got married and left off playing with sheep. So the king said he would arrange a grand tournament. The tournament was to last three days, and all the princes and the nobles and the knights from round about were to compete. The prizes were to be three pots of flowers, and the winner was to have the princess for his wife.

'But I don't want to marry any of your lords or knights!' pouted the princess.

'You'll do as I say, my lady!' said the king. 'For this time I am—*I am* putting my royal foot down!' And he stamped that royal foot, and went off to arrange about the tournament. So the princess ran to the young shepherd. 'Shepherd boy, shepherd boy, it's *you* I want to marry! Come to the tournament tomorrow at nine o'clock, and try—oh do try—to win a pot of flowers!'

And the young shepherd promised he would come.

So next morning, very early, before the princess was awake, the young shepherd led the sheep to the meadow, left them there to look after themselves and went to the steel castle. He dressed himself all in steel armour, put a steel helmet on his head with the vizor pulled down over his face to hide it, jumped onto the steel horse, and off with him galloping to the tournament. He fought long and he fought well, he unhorsed all those who came against him, and before the day was done, he had gained the first pot of flowers. And with that pot of flowers he galloped fast off the field.

'Ah,' said the king, 'what a brave knight! I hope he will come again tomorrow! I should like *him* to win my daughter!'

The princess ran in tears to the meadow. There was the young shepherd, sitting among the sheep, playing his whistle.

'Why didn't you come, oh why didn't you?' sobbed the princess.

She sobbed and she scolded: she slapped him in her temper. The young shepherd laughed. But he promised he would come next day.

And he did come next day. He came in silver armour on a silver horse, and no one knew him. He fought hard, he fought long, he unhorsed all his adversaries, and rode away with the second pot of flowers. And before he rode away the king said to him, 'Come again tomorrow, my brave knight. I hope it is *you* who will win my daughter.'

For the silver knight was even more to the king's liking than the steel one had been.

Oh how the princess stormed and wept when she went that evening to the meadow and found her shepherd boy lazing there among the sheep. 'You promised to come and you never came!' she cried. 'I hate you! I hate you! I won't marry anybody ever!'

Said he, 'What should a shepherd lad do among all those great lords? They would laugh me to scorn.'

'I will lend you some of my father's clothes!' said the princess.

But no, he wouldn't dress up in any of the king's clothes. All the same, he promised to come next morning.

So, next morning, there were all the lords and nobles and knights prancing about on the tournament field, and there were the king and the queen and the princess seated on a dais under the embroidered canopy to watch the contests. And it was nine o'clock and time for the tournament to begin.

Among the riders was a knight in gold armour, riding a golden horse. 'Ah, superb!' cried the king. 'The steel knight was good, the silver knight was better, but the gold knight is best of all! I pray that *he* may be the conqueror, and win you for his bride, my daughter!'

But the princess was looking everywhere for her shepherd boy. She couldn't see him. 'Papa, papa,' she cried, 'let us wait one little half-hour!'

'Very well,' said the king.

And they waited.

But the half-hour passed, and still no shepherd boy.

'Papa, papa, let us wait till ten o'clock!'

'Very well,' said the king.

And they waited.

Ten o'clock! Still no shepherd boy—

'Papa, papa, let us wait a little longer!'

'Very well, we will wait till eleven o'clock, but no longer.'

They waited till eleven o'clock. Still no shepherd boy. The princes and the nobles and the knights were getting impatient, the horses were champing at their bits. 'We won't wait another minute,' said the king. 'It isn't my fault if your shepherd boy doesn't want to come.'

He gave a sign with his hand, and the tournament began.

The princess sat on the royal dais under the embroidered

canopy with her eyes shut. She wouldn't watch the tournament. So she didn't see how the gold knight unhorsed his rivals one after another. But she couldn't help hearing the shouts of the watching crowd, or the delighted remarks of the king. 'Ah! See the gold hero, how he knocks the rest about like ninepins! Ah ha—there goes the last of them! The steel knight was good, the silver knight was better, but the gold knight is the best of all!'

So, in the afternoon, when all the other champions had been defeated, the gold knight rode up to the king and received the last pot of flowers.

'My son-in-law! My son-in-law!' cried the king. 'Let down your vizor that I may embrace you!'

'Sire, I cannot stay,' answered the gold knight. 'I will come again tomorrow.'

And he set spurs to his horse, and galloped off the field.

That evening the princess went weeping to the meadow. There was the young shepherd sitting among the sheep, playing merry tunes on his whistle.

'Shepherd boy, shepherd boy,' wept the princess. 'It is you I want to marry, but tomorrow my father will give me to the gold knight.'

'Come with me,' said the shepherd boy, and he took her into the first wood. He showed her the dead giant, he took her into the steel stable and showed her the steel horse; he took her into the steel castle, and there on a steel table stood the first pot of flowers.

He took her into the second wood. He showed her the dead giant, he showed her the silver stable and the silver horse; he took her into the silver castle, and there on a silver table stood the second pot of flowers.

He took her into the third wood, he showed her the dead giant; he took her to the gold stable and showed her the gold horse; he took her into the gold castle, and there on a gold table stood the third pot of flowers.

'And now,' said he laughing, 'have I won you for my wife?'

The princess laughed also. 'Yes,' said she, 'if you are not too rich and grand?'

'I am very rich and very grand, if you love me,' said he.

'I love you with all my heart,' said the princess.

So the shepherd boy went to the king, taking with him the three pots of flowers. The king laughed like anything to think how he had been taken in. But he consented to the wedding, so the princess got her way as usual. The princess rode to church on the gold horse, and the shepherd rode on the silver one. And next day they buried the three giants, and turned the steel horse and the silver horse and the gold horse out to graze in the meadow of the three woods.

As to the flock of sheep—well, the princess gave all those sheep away: she didn't seem to want to be bothered with them any longer.

The Prince of the Seven Golden Cows

There once lived a rich and generous prince whom everyone called the Prince of the Seven Golden Cows, because he had seven golden cows painted on a shield at the gate of his castle. Every morning this prince stood at the gate of his castle and gave away money and clothes and meat and drink to all in need; every evening he sat down to dine with a hundred friends, and those hundred friends went away loaded with presents. So that both rich and poor fawned on him and said, 'Prince of the Seven Golden Cows, your like is not born. For you we would go through fire and water!'

Now one day it so happened that the prince was sitting alone, thinking; and there came to him a young man dressed in black and weeping bitter tears.

'Friend,' said the prince, 'what ails you, and how can I help you?'

And the young man answered, 'Oh my prince, I loved a maiden and thought soon to make her my wife. But fever came to her home; her father died, her mother died, her brother died; last of all the fever took her, and this morning she also died. And I—oh me, what shall I do?—I have not money enough to bury her.'

Then the prince filled a purse with gold and gave it to the young man: and the young man, having knelt and embraced the knees of the prince, went away to bury his sweetheart.

In three days the young man came again, and said, 'Prince of the Seven Golden Cows, let me be your servant! I will serve you faithfully all my life, and I will serve you without wages.'

'Nay friend,' said the prince, 'that must not be. A man is worthy of his hire.'

'Prince of the Seven Golden Cows, I will serve you for love, or not at all.'

And the prince, seeing that this was what the young man really desired, took him into his service, and fed and clothed him, but paid him nothing.

And the young man, who never ceased to wear mourning for his dead sweetheart, became known as the Black Valet.

The Black Valet served the prince diligently; he studied him in all things, he watched, he listened; he stood at the prince's elbow when he gave alms to the poor, he stood behind the prince's chair when he feasted with his friends; he heard the cry of both rich and poor repeated many, many times, 'Prince of the Seven Golden Cows, your like is not yet born. For you we would go through fire and water!'

Very soon the Black Valet knew more of the prince's affairs than any other living soul.

And one day when the prince was again sitting alone, the Black Valet came to him and said, 'Prince of the Seven Golden Cows, you are living beyond your means; you are squandering your wealth on fawners and flatterers: on those who love you only for your gold. If you continue to live thus—in another month I shall see you in the gutter.'

But the prince laughed and said, 'Black Valet, what nonsense are you talking! My friends will never let me lack!'

And the Black Valet answered, 'Prince of the Seven Golden Cows, your so-called friends deceive you.'

That night, when as usual the Prince of the Seven Golden Cows was feasting with his hundred friends, and the Black Valet as usual stood behind his chair, the prince sent the valet out of the banqueting hall on an errand, and when the valet had gone, the prince stood up and asked for silence, and said to the assembled company, 'Are you my friends?'

'Are we your friends!' cry one and all. 'Prince of the Seven Golden Cows, how can you ask us? Your like is not born! For you we would go through fire and water!'

'But,' said the prince, 'my valet tells me I am deceived in you.'

Then what an uproar! 'The Black Valet indeed! The Black Valet is a rascal! It is he, the Black Valet, that deceives you! Ah, we know it! Yes, we have seen it with our own eyes. The Black Valet steals from you! Prince of the Seven Golden Cows, for whom we would go through fire and water, the Black Valet has made away with enough of your gold to buy a fine water-mill! Yes, and a house with woods! Yes, and seven farms! Ask him, charge him with it! He cannot deny it!'

'I will ask him,' said the prince.

No more was said. The hundred guests finished their feasting and went away, as usual, loaded with presents.

And when they were gone the prince called the Black Valet to him, and told him what his friends had said. 'But there is some mistake,' he said. 'I cannot believe it!'

And the Black Valet answered quietly, 'My Prince, you can believe it, for it is true. With gold from your treasury I have bought a water-mill. With gold from your treasury I have bought a house and woods. With gold from your treasury I have bought seven farms.'

Then the prince put his hands before his face and wept. 'Go, go from my sight,' he said. 'Let me never see you again!'

And the Black Valet went away from the castle that very night.

The prince went on giving alms to the poor, he went on feasting his hundred friends, but he mourned in secret for his faithless servant. And one day there came to the castle two unwelcome visitors, the bailiff and the sheriff. 'Prince of the Seven Golden Cows,' said they, 'you are in debt to persons innumerable. All your wealth you have squandered; there is nothing left. We have come to take possession of your castle and all your goods.'

Then the prince summoned his friends, and told them his trouble. 'Lend me now enough to pay my debts,' said he, 'and when my fortune mends I will repay you.'

Lend him money indeed! Not they! Ah the braggart! He had ruined himself showing off, giving alms to the poor! Well then, let the poor now help him!

And they jeered at him and insulted him.

The prince left them sadly enough. He went out to the gate of his castle. What did he see there? A crowd of beggars shouting and mocking him. 'Good day, Prince of the Empty Purse! Your servants have refused us even a scrap of bread! They say they have no bread, they threaten to set the dogs on us. Prince of the Empty Purse, you who have revelled with your flatterers and gluttons, now you are an outcast like ourselves!'

And they picked up stones to stone him.

But hark! The sound of galloping hoofs and a loud barking of dogs. Ah, now who comes galloping full speed on a great horse, oak staff in hand, and with a pack of huge hounds running behind him? Who but the Black Valet! He sends that rascally crowd flying in all directions; the prince's fine friends who had come out to see the fun, make off as fast as may be. And when everyone has gone, the Black Valet gets down from his horse and kneels at the prince's feet.

'Prince of the Seven Golden Cows, my dear, dear master, I have come to take you to the home I have prepared for you. It was for this I took gold from your treasury, that I might have a home for you when you had squandered all.'

So the prince got up on the valet's horse, and the valet walked beside him, and the pack of dogs followed at the horse's heels, and they went away to the house that the valet had bought with gold from the prince's treasury.

And in that house the prince lived for seven years; and the Black Valet served him faithfully.

And then, one evening, the prince called the Black Valet to him and said, 'Black Valet, you who alone have kept faith with me, I am going to tell you a great secret. I might long ago have been as rich as before, but I wished to test my so-called friends—and you know how they served me. Black Valet, I am not called the Prince of the Seven Golden Cows merely because of a picture painted on a shield. Those seven golden cows both live and breathe, my friend, and it is from them that my wealth springs. Now that I am growing old and must soon die, I would teach you to play the flute, that you may learn the tune that will call my seven golden cows out of the earth. Go then, fetch a hatchet, and saddle two horses; but make haste, for we have a long way to ride before midnight.'

The Black Valet, greatly wondering, fetched a hatchet, saddled two horses, and galloped off with the prince. They galloped, galloped in the light of the moon, and at midnight they came to the borders of a pool filled up with great reeds.

'Here we dismount,' said the prince. 'And Black Valet, if you would live, you must do from point to point all that I say. In this pool do you see one reed that is larger than all the other reeds?'

'Yes, master, I see it.'

'Black Valet, you must take the hatchet and cut that reed close to the root. The reed will try to defy you: it will change its shape three times and make you see things which are not. Take no heed: whatever shape you see, cut it down, cut it down. If at your third stroke the reed is not cut down, the earth will swallow you alive; and neither I nor any man will see you again.'

'Prince of the Seven Golden Cows, I will obey you in all things.'

Then the Black Valet waded into the pool and laid the hatchet to the reed close to the root. Immediately the reed turned into a seven-headed serpent. It hissed from its seven open mouths, and darted fire from its seven tongues. But the Black Valet cut it down. No sooner was it cut down than it changed into a little naked infant: but the Black Valet hardened his heart and cut it down. Then for a third time that reed changed, and this time—ah! ah!—it changed into a young girl, the very image of the Black Valet's dead sweetheart. The Black Valet sobbed and trembled—could he cut *her* down? Yes he could, he must, he *did* cut her down: and lo! there lay the reed cut off to its very root.

So the Black Valet came out of the pool and gave the reed to his master, and they got on their horses and rode home together. And the prince made the reed into a flute, and taught the Black Valet the tune that would call the seven golden cows up from the earth.

So it came midsummer eve and moonlight, and the prince bade the Black Valet saddle the horses again and put the flute in his pocket: and the prince himself fetched two big cauldrons and seven strong hempen sacks. Then, having loaded these things onto the horses, the prince and the Black Valet rode off together over hill, over dale, till they came to a great river, and there they dismounted.

'Black Valet,' said the prince, 'put the flute to your lips, and play the tune I have taught you.'

Then the Black Valet put the flute to his lips and played the tune the prince had taught him. And lo, before the notes of the tune had died away, seven golden cows rose out of the ground. And each cow bowed her head before the prince, and then went to graze on the grass by the banks of the river in the moonlight.

'Black Valet,' said the prince, 'bring here the two cauldrons, and whilst you milk one cow, I will milk another.'

And they knelt and milked two cows into the cauldrons; and each drop of milk that fell into the cauldrons changed into a gold coin. And they milked till the cauldrons were full to the brim. Then the prince emptied the gold coins into two of the sacks, tied up the mouths of the sacks, and threw them into the river. And after that they milked two more cows, and then two more, and then the Black Valet milked the last one. And as before, so now—the milk turned into gold coins, and the gold coins filled the cauldrons: two cauldrons full, and two cauldrons full and two cauldrons full, and lastly one cauldron full; and each time the prince poured the gold coins into the sacks, and flung the sacks into the river. Before sunrise all the cows were milked, seven sacks full of gold lay on the river bed, and the seven golden cows bowed before the prince and went back under the earth.

'Black Valet,' said the prince then, 'you know where the seven sacks are. I give them to you. Fish them up at your need, but let none see you. And when the gold is all spent, you can call the cows again. And now, my faithful friend, we will ride home, for I am old and weary, I shall not ride my good horse again; nor shall I see another moon at the full.'

And it was as the prince said: before the moon had come to the full again, he died.

The Black Valet buried the prince with all honour, and mourned for many days. And then he called to him a company of heralds and sent them with a proclamation throughout the country round about the prince's former castle: the castle where the prince had once stood at the gate giving alms to the thankless poor, and where he had once feasted his faithless friends:

'Oyez! Oyez! Oyez! The Prince of the Seven Golden Cows is dead. The Black Valet is his heir. But the Prince of the Seven Golden Cows has left a fine legacy to each of his old friends and to each poor person in the country. Tomorrow morning, outside the castle gate, all will be paid.'

Next morning there was such a gathering of old friends and

poor outside the castle gate that the place was like a fair. 'Ah, heaven bless the Prince of the Seven Golden Cows!' cried one and all. 'May his soul rest in peace! Never more shall we see his like on earth! For him we would have gone through fire and water! He did not forget his old friends, he did not forget the poor at his gates: he has left us each a legacy. . . . And see, there at full gallop comes his messenger, laden with the gifts he has left for us!'

It was the Black Valet who galloped up to them, stout oak staff in hand, followed by a pack of huge dogs, bringing the legacies he had promised them. But not such legacies as they expected:

'Scoundrels, fawners, time-servers, false, false miscreants!' cried the Black Valet. 'Here are the legacies the Prince of the Seven Golden Cows has left you, and well you deserve them!'

And so shouting, the Black Valet galloped among the crowd, hitting out right and left with his stout oak staff, whilst the huge dogs ran growling and snapping, tripping people up, and tearing the clothes from their backs. Sprawling, panting, screaming, bruised and beaten the crowd fled in all directions. The Black Valet called his dogs to heel; then he dismounted and stood at the great gate of the castle, where the shield, painted with the images of the seven golden cows, hung awry and covered with dust.

After the shouting and the screaming and the barking of dogs, all was silent. The Black Valet bowed before the shield. 'Prince of the Seven Golden Cows, my dear, dear master,' said he, 'I have avenged your wrongs.'

There was nothing left for the Black Valet to do, but to go home. Yet still he stood before the castle gate, looking up at the painted shield. Now that his rage had died out of him, he he felt very sad, very lonely. . . .

What was that? Somebody sighing? Surely, surely, no one is left here? Surely the Black Valet is all alone?

No, the Black Valet is not alone. There, half hidden by a pillar of the great gate stands a young girl. The young girl looks sadly at the Black Valet, and her eyes are like the eyes of his dead sweetheart, only those eyes are filled with tears.

'Little one—who are you?'

'Sir, I am a poor orphan. Sir, I am very hungry. Sir, I came here thinking to receive a coin to buy bread. But I found no coin and no bread—only blows and misery.'

Then the Black Valet's heart was stirred with love and pity. 'Little one, you look at me with the eyes of my dead sweetheart. Little one, those eyes shall shed no more tears. Come with me—you shall be rich and happy!'

So the Black Valet set the young girl up before him on his horse. And he took her to his home, and married her.

The Sword of the Stone

There was a good king who had a good queen and a little son of seven years old. They were beloved and happy, all three. But there was also the terrible king of the pagans, a huge man whom neither iron nor steel could wound or kill. And the king of the pagans made war against our good king and killed him.

When the good queen heard that her king was killed, she called her little son to her and said, 'Little son, we are now in the power of the king of the pagans. And so that this terrible king of the pagans shall not kill you also, my little one, you must pretend to be deaf and dumb and stupid. Then he will think you worthless and let you live. Remember never, never to speak to me unless I first say to you, "We are now alone, quite, quite alone."'

'Mother,' said the little prince, 'I will remember.'

Then the queen dressed herself in a robe the colour of the moon, took her little son by the hand, and went down to meet the king of the pagans at the palace gate. She was so beautiful, so beautiful, that the king of the pagans said, 'Queen, I am now master of this country. Queen, I love you, you must become my wife.'

'King of the pagans,' said the poor queen, 'you shall be obeyed.'

'Queen,' said the king of the pagans, 'is this your child?'

'Yes, king of the pagans, but he is a poor unfortunate and worth nothing, for he is deaf and dumb and witless.'

The king of the pagans was suspicious, and said to the child, 'Little one, it was I who killed your father.'

The child stared at him stupidly and said nothing.

But the king of the pagans was still suspicious.

'Little one, I am going to kill *you*.'

The child stared at him stupidly and said nothing.

But the king of the pagans was still suspicious.

'Little one, I am going to kill your mother.'

Still the child stared at him stupidly and said nothing.

So then the king of the pagans thought, 'I am quite safe. That stupid deaf-mute is no danger to me. What is he but half a fool? He will never have wits enough to think of avenging his father.'

And so, having forced the unhappy queen to marry him, he let the child live. But he drove away all the queen's attendants, and filled the palace with his own followers.

How this poor unhappy queen wept, wept in secret! And sometimes, when the king of the pagans was out hunting, she would beckon the little prince to her and whisper, 'Little son, now we are alone, quite, quite alone. When you grow big and strong do not forget all that I have suffered for you.'

And the little prince would whisper, 'Mother, I will never, never forget!'

For seven years the prince lived at the court, acting deaf and dumb and witless; mocked and scorned by the pagan king and all his followers, and avoided, it seemed, even by his mother. But on the day after the prince's fourteenth birthday, when the king of the pagans and his followers had set out on a grand hunting expedition, the queen beckoned the prince up to her room, locked the door, and whispered, 'My son, now that we are alone, quite, quite alone, I have something to tell you. It is true that neither iron nor tempered steel can wound or kill the pagan king. There is only one weapon in all the world that can kill him, and that is the Sword of the Stone. But the Sword of the Stone has lain hidden these hundreds of years, and none knows the place where it is hidden. Here is a purse of money. Take it and go quickly out into the world. Seek the Sword of the Stone, so that when you are big and strong you may avenge your father's death, and our bitter sorrow. And if ever you can—send me news in secret.'

And the prince answered, 'Mother, I will find that sword. And if I can I will send you news in secret.'

Then, having knelt for his mother's blessing, he went from the palace.

When the pagan king came back from the hunt he said, 'Queen, where is that fool son of yours?'

'It seems he has run away,' said the queen. 'No doubt one day we shall hear that he has been found dead in a ditch. Perhaps that will be no great loss?'

'But oh my son, my son,' she thought, 'may heaven preserve you!'

The young prince walked on and on for a whole year, but nowhere could he get tidings of the Sword of the Stone. So at last he came to the edge of the sea, in a country of great oaks and pasture-lands. By this time his shoes were worn out and his purse was empty; so, seeing close at hand a large farm-house, he knocked at the door and asked if the farmer could give him work.

'Well,' said the farmer, 'I need a shepherd to guard my flock of three hundred sheep, some white, some black, on the edge of this great sea. But he must be a strong lad and brave, for wolves abound.'

'Master,' said the prince, 'I am but fifteen years old. But I am strong and fearless. Master, let me be your shepherd!'

The farmer agreed to give the prince a trial. He took him in, set food before him, and showed him where he could sleep.

Next morning the prince rose at dawn, whistled to the farmer's dogs, opened the gate of the sheepfold and led out the flock of three hundred sheep, some white, some black, which he went to guard in the pastures on the edge of the great sea. In the evening he came back, driving his flock, and carrying on his shoulders three dead wolves.

'Master, here is your flock of three hundred sheep, some

white, some black; not one is missing. And here are three dead wolves; I have wrung their necks like chickens.'

'Shepherd,' said the farmer, 'you are a lad after my own heart!'

The next day, the same thing. And so for many days. The prince and his dogs between them killed so many wolves that by and by no more dared approach to worry the flock. And the prince's days were peaceful.

Now it came summertime and very hot; and one day, at noon, the prince felt sleepy. So, bidding his dogs keep watch, he lay down under the shade of a big oak tree and closed his eyes.

And clinging to the trunk of the oak tree was a woodpecker, bitterly complaining:

Quiou, quiou, quiou!

'Woodpecker,' said the prince, 'you bore me to death! I wish to sleep. Why are you so full of complaints?'

'*Quiou, quiou, quiou!* Shepherd, I have good reason to complain. The hornets have driven me from the nest I had hollowed out in the trunk of this old oak.'

'Patience, woodpecker, I will give you back your nest!'

Then the prince struck a light with his tinder-box, lit a handful of dry grass, and smoked the hornets out of the nest. 'Here, woodpecker, go back to your nest, and don't bore me any more with your complaints. I wish to sleep.'

'*Quiou, quiou, quiou!* Shepherd, you have done me a great service. I will repay you according to my power. Shepherd, I know who you are. I know what you think of night and day. You think of your mother, the queen, who said to you, "Go out into the world, find the Sword of the Stone, that when you are big and strong you may avenge your father's death, and our bitter sorrow. Send me news in secret when you can, and do not forget what I suffer for you." Shepherd, I don't know where the Sword of the Stone may be, but if you wish news taken in secret to your mother, speak, and you shall be obeyed.'

And the prince said, 'Go, woodpecker. Say to my mother, "Your son is well. On the borders of the great sea he keeps a flock of three hundred sheep, some white, some black. And he does not forget what you suffer for him."'

Whizz! Off goes the woodpecker like a bullet shot from a gun. *Whizz! Whizz!* At sunset he reached the palace of the pagan king, found the queen's window, and pecked at the closed shutter. All night he was pecking with his long sharp beak at the shutter, and by morning he had made a hole in it. So, in with him through the hole, finds the queen in bed and all alone, and goes to perch on the bed-rail.

'*Quiou, quiou, quiou!* Good morning, queen! Your son is well. On the borders of the great sea he keeps a flock of three hundred sheep, some white, some black. He bids me say that he does not forget what you suffer for him.'

'Thank you, thank you, woodpecker! Fly back to my son and take him my undying love.'

Whizz! Off goes the woodpecker again like a bullet shot from a gun. *Whizz! Whizz!* By sunset he is back on the borders of the great sea, where the prince is keeping his flock.

'*Quiou, quiou, quiou!* Shepherd, I have delivered your message to the queen your mother. And I bring you her undying love.'

'Thank you, thank you, woodpecker! From now on I think we shall be great friends.'

And the prince and the woodpecker became great friends; from sunrise to sunset they chatted together. But one day the woodpecker flew into a rage.

'*Quiou, quiou, quiou!* Shepherd, now for a whole year you have been idling on the border of this great sea, keeping your flock of three hundred sheep, some white, some black. Shepherd, at this rate you will never find the Sword of the Stone! Go, wander through the world. If you have need of me again, you know what I have promised.'

'Woodpecker, you are right!' The prince jumped to his feet, whistled to his dogs, rounded up his sheep, and set about driving them back to the farm. 'Good-bye, woodpecker! Tomorrow night I shall be far away!'

That night the prince said to the farmer, 'Tomorrow I must leave you. I have urgent business elsewhere.'

The farmer was sorry to part with him. He gave the prince a good handful of money. And next morning the prince went from the farm.

He walked, walked, walked from sunrise to sunset. He walked for a whole year, but nowhere could he get news of the Sword of the Stone. So one morning he was going across a moor, and he was hungry, and sat down on a stone to eat the bread he carried in his knapsack. It was summertime again, the ground was dry and cracked, and seven lizards came out of the earth and began licking up the crumbs that fell from the bread.

But the prince said, 'Eat little lizards, eat my little friends! Here is the rest of my bread!' And he threw them all of the loaf that he had not yet eaten.

'*Tziou, tziou, tziou!* Young man, you have done us great service. Young man, we know who you are; we know that you seek the Sword of the Stone, that you may kill the pagan king, and avenge your father's death and your mother's bitter sorrow. Young man, we don't know where the Sword of the Stone may be. But we know that on Christmas night, when you are far far from us, you will get news of that sword. But that will not be the end of your troubles. So if ever you have need of us, whistle loudly, *Tziou, tziou, tziou*. Then, wherever we are, and whatever we may be doing, we will leave all and come to your aid.'

'Thank you, my lizards. Good-bye, my lizards.'

The prince walks on. He walks, walks, walks. He walks through the rest of the summer, he walks through the quiet days of autumn, he walks through the cold days of early winter, but nowhere can he get news of the Sword of the Stone. And now it was the night of Christmas, the moon shone brilliantly, and the ground was white with snow. The prince thought, 'The time spoken of by the lizards has come. But I have yet no news of the Sword of the Stone.'

At midnight he came to the banks of a shallow river; and there on the bank stood an old, old man, shivering with cold and gazing helplessly at the water. And the prince went up to him:

'Good evening, poor old man! It is surely bad weather for travelling! And it is surely bad to shiver with cold! I have wine here in my gourd. Drink it! It will warm you.'

The old man took a long drink from the gourd. He stopped shivering. 'Thank you, friend! But I must cross this river, and my poor old legs sink under me. Take me on your back and carry me over, I entreat you!'

'With pleasure, old man! Up on my back, and hold tight .... Why, you weigh no more than a feather!'

'Young sir, I shall weigh more in the middle of the stream.'

The prince laughs, he doesn't believe it. He steps into the water and begins to carry the old man across. But at every step the prince takes, the old man gets heavier and heavier. By the time he is in the middle of the river, the prince can hardly stagger, his breath comes in gasps, his back bows, his legs shake and sway, it seems that every bone in his body must be crushed to powder:

'Heavens, old man, you spoke truly!'

'Patience, young sir, when we approach the farther shore I shall weigh no more than a feather.'

And it was as the old man said. With every step the prince took from the middle of the river, his burden grew lighter and lighter; and when he set the old man down on the farther shore, it seemed that he set down such a slight load that he laughed.

'Old man,' says he, 'here you are over, safe and sound. Drink another draught from my gourd; then go on your way, poor old man, and may God go with you!'

'Young sir, do you call *me* poor old man? That is not at all what I am! I am a wizard of no mean power. You have done me great service, and I will reward you according to my ability. Young man, I know who you are, and what you seek. Now listen to me. Until daybreak take your way along the river bank. When the sun rises you will see before you a great black hole, a hole a hundred fathoms deep. Courage, courage! Go down into that hole without fear or trembling. Go down to the very bottom, helping yourself with your hands and feet. But when you reach the bottom you will not be at the end of your troubles. Long, very long, you will travel underground. In your knapsack you will find every day enough bread and meat not to die of hunger. In your gourd you will find every day enough wine not to die of thirst. Be careful not to eat or drink anything else. And walk on, walk on. At last you will come to a great cave, where seven hundred lamps and seven hundred candles burn night and day. In the middle of the cave stands a white stone; and thrust into that stone is the sword you seek. If you have kept faith, and done as I bid you do, you will be able to draw the sword out of the stone.'

The prince and the king of the owls from
The Son of the King of Spain

The prince had hardly time to thank the old man, before that old man vanished.

So the prince walked on by the river. It was cold, very cold. The moon went down: it was dark, very dark. There was nothing to guide him but the gurgle and darkness of the water, flowing between the faint glimmer of the snow-covered banks. But at last the sun came up, round and red. And there at his feet the prince saw a huge dark hole.

And into that huge dark hole he leaped, and down he went, and down, and down, a hundred fathoms down, clutching with hands, scrambling with feet amongst clefts and chinks and jutting rocks that he could not see, till at last he touched bottom, and found himself standing on a broad road. And in the middle of the road was a table spread with food and drink: and at the table sat a crowd of gaily-dressed boys and girls, eating and drinking.

When these boys and girls saw the prince, they jumped up and ran to meet him, crying out, 'Welcome friend, welcome! Come, you are weary and hungry and travel-stained! Come, eat and drink with us! Come, rest with us!'

The prince was sorely tempted; for he *was* tired and hungry and travel-stained, and the boys and girls seemed so friendly, and the food they were holding out to him looked so delicious. But he remembered in time what the old man had told him: he struck the food and drink from their hands; he overturned their table. 'Be off, scum!' he shouted.

And at once they all vanished, and the table vanished.

The prince walked on, he walked long and long, he lost all count of time, for there was no day nor night down there, but always a grey twilight. When he was hungry he found food in his knapsack, when he was thirsty he found wine in his gourd, just enough to satisfy him and no more.

On and on and on; with nothing to see before or behind but the broad road flanked by high cliffs; with nothing to hear but the sound of his own footsteps. And then, all at once, he heard a wailing cry, 'Ah! Ah! Ah! Ah!' and there at the side

of the road lay a man with carroty hair and green eyes; and
the bones were showing through his flesh, and his flesh was
showing through the rags that covered him.

'What is the matter then, poor friend?' said the prince.

'Ah! Ah! Ah! Ah! I can no longer put one foot before the
other. I hunger, I thirst! Help me, help me! For pity's sake,
young man, get me out of here!'

The prince stooped and put his gourd to the man's lips; he
gave him meat and bread from his knapsack; he helped him to
his feet. 'Come, give me your arm, poor friend. We will walk
on together. I will get you out of here.'

So on they walked together. They walked long and long,
seeing no living creature but their two selves. When they
hungered, they found just enough food in the knapsack to
satisfy them both. When they thirsted they found just enough
wine in the gourd to slake their thirst. The prince would know
how his companion came there; but the man only laughed as
if he were crazed, and would tell him nothing.

And so at last the road ended, the cliff walls closed in, and
there, barring their way, was a huge iron door. The door had
three bolts, the prince pushed them back, and swung the door
open. Inside was an immense cave, lit by seven hundred lamps
and seven hundred candles. In the middle of the cave stood a
white stone. And thrust into that stone up to its golden hilt,
was a sword.

The prince ran, he grasped the hilt with both hands, he
pulled out the sword. 'I have it! I have it!' he shouted to his
companion. 'See, see! The Sword of the Stone!'

But there was no answer. His companion wasn't there. He
had stolen out of the cave. What was he doing? He was shoot-
ing the three bolts of the door into their sockets. 'Ha! Ha! Ha!'
he laughed. 'You wanted the Sword of the Stone! Well,
you have it! Now try to get out of here!'

Oh me! Oh me! Betrayed! The prince hammered at the
door with all his might. He ran at it. He beat it with his fists,
kicked it with his feet. 'Open! Open!' But he got no answer

except a fiendish laughter. And the laughter went farther and farther away . . .

And then there was silence.

What to do? The prince sat down with the sword between his knees, and thought, thought. Then he jumped up and called the woodpecker. *'Quiou, quiou, quiou!* Friend, you who promised to help me, come, come to my aid!'

But the woodpecker did not come.

Then the prince put his fingers to his lips and whistled loudly, calling the lizards. *'Tziou, tziou, tziou!* Little friends, little lizards, you who said "wherever we are, whatever we may be doing, call us and we will leave all and come to you"— come, come, come to my aid!'

But the lizards did not come.

For a whole year the prince remained shut in that huge cave, lit night and day by the seven hundred lamps and the seven hundred candles that shone only on his misery. But the bread and the meat in his knapsack, and the wine in his gourd, did not fail him.

And then one morning, as he sat bowed in wretchedness, with the Sword of the Stone between his knees, he heard, under the ground at his feet, a tiny sound: *Tziou, tziou, tziou.* It was the seven lizards, and they were working, working, working down there. Soon they had a tiny hole in the ground, and by and by they had a great hole; and there they were, all seven of them, scampering round the prince's feet and chattering:

'Tziou, tziou, tziou! Friend, we heard your call. But it has taken us a whole year to dig a passage to you under the earth. Quick now, take the Sword of the Stone, and come!'

The lizards led the prince through the passage they had made, up and up for three days, till he stood once more on the blessed earth, with the blue sky above him, and the sun shining.

'Good-bye, little lizards! Good-bye, my good little friends! Thank you, thank you, little lizards!'

'Good-bye, good-bye, prince!'

The lizards scampered off. The prince put his hand to his lips and called loudly. *Quiou, quiou, quiou!*

Whizz! There came the woodpecker, flying like a cannon-ball.

'*Quiou, quiou, quiou!* Prince, I heard your call a year ago. But how could I reach you under the earth?'

'Woodpecker, all that matters is that you are here now. Fly to the queen, my mother. Tell her that her son has ceased to wander about the world. He has found the Sword of the Stone. He is coming to avenge his father's death, and her bitter sorrow.'

Whizz! Off went the woodpecker, swift as a cannon-ball. The queen got her message. She waited joyfully, joyfully. For a whole year she waited. And then one day a man, dressed as a pilgrim, knocked at the palace door.

Rat, tat, tat! 'Serving-men go tell the queen there is a pilgrim here, selling beautiful medals of gold and silver.'

The serving-men took the message. The queen said, 'Let him come up.'

The prince went up to the queen's room. He drew aside the folds of his pilgrim's robe. He showed the Sword of the Stone, hanging at his belt.

'We are alone, quite, quite alone,' whispered the queen.

'Mother,' said the prince, 'I have done with wandering about the world. I have found the Sword of the Stone. I have not forgotten what you have suffered for me. Where is the king of the pagans?'

'My son, he is out hunting in the forest. In one hour he will return.'

'Mother, in one hour the king of the pagans will have finished doing evil.'

The prince flung off his pilgrim's robe, snatched up a shield, ran to the stables, saddled and bridled the swiftest horse there, galloped off to the forest and found the king of the pagans.

'Ho! King of the pagans! I am the deaf-mute. I have found

the Sword of the Stone. I come to avenge my father's death and my mother's bitter sorrow. King of the pagans, defend yourself!'

The king of the pagans roars with rage and gallops to meet the prince. Their shields clash together. Ho, king of the pagans, you may be huge, you may be terrible, you may be very, very strong, but with one thrust of the Sword of the Stone, the prince has severed your head from your body!

Then the prince took possession of his father's kingdom. He governed well. He cherished his mother. He married a princess of excellent beauty; and by and by they had three lovely children. Then the poor sad queen mother so rejoiced in her grandchildren that the end of her life was happy.

The Son of the King of Spain

There was once an elderly king whose wife died, leaving him with a baby daughter. The king felt very lonely and very sad. But he thought, 'At least I have a little daughter to keep me company.'

So year followed year, and there was the little princess growing up, and there was the king getting older and older. And one day he thought, 'Heaven help me! The princess will soon be wanting me to find a husband for her. And when I *have* found a husband for her—what will she do? She will go away with him. And there I shall be, left all alone!'

And he fell into an angry despair, thinking of the imaginary prince who would some day carry off his daughter. And he said to himself, 'No, I won't let anyone have her! I will be cunning. I will let all the world know that I seek a husband for my daughter. But on every suitor that comes asking for her hand, I will impose three such terrible tasks that the suitor will lose his life in trying to accomplish them.'

And he let it be known far and wide that he sought a husband for the princess.

Now the princess was renowned for her sweetness and her beauty. So from all the neighbouring countries princes and great lords came seeking her hand. But when the king told them of the three tasks they must perform to prove themselves worthy of her, all those princes and great lords rode off again. 'We grant,' said they, 'that the princess is very beautiful and very charming; but there are other beautiful and charming maidens in the world. So why should we lose our lives for the sake of this one?'

The king rubbed his hands and chuckled. And as for the princess, she didn't mind. She hadn't taken a particular fancy to any of those suitors who came so eagerly and rode away so swiftly. She laughed and sang and teased the ageing king, telling him that she would be an old maid and live with him forever.

But one morning the princess looked out of her window, and what did she see? A young man on a great white horse riding in through the palace gate. And he rode so gallantly, and when he looked up and saw her he bowed so pleasantly, and he had such a frank and merry face that the princess's heart gave a little hop and flew out to him. 'Oh, oh,' said she, hiding herself behind the window curtain, 'this one is quite, quite different! If *he* goes away I believe I shall cry. Yes, I'm sure I shall cry!'

So when this young man asked to see the king and was led into the king's presence, what did the princess do but go to listen behind the door.

'Sire,' said the young man, 'I am a prince, the son of the King of Spain, and I come to ask the hand of your daughter in marriage.'

Said the king, 'If you are worthy of her, you shall have her. But how do I know that you are worthy?'

'Set me to the proof, sire,' said the prince.

'Very well,' said the king. 'Bring me here the wine that gives youth, the wine that is guarded by a great scaly monster who never sleeps, in the middle of a thicket of thorn trees. Bring me here also the head of an ogre that lives in the forest on the borders of my kingdom. Bring me here also the breastplate that is worn by the ogre, a breastplate that is proof against sword-thrust, bullet and cannon-ball—bring me these three things and you shall have my daughter.'

'Sire, you shall be obeyed,' said the son of the King of Spain, bowing low. And he walked proudly out from the king's presence.

The princess had skipped away from behind the door. When

the son of the King of Spain went out of the palace, there she was walking in the garden. 'Son of the King of Spain,' said she, 'I don't want you to die for me!'

'I shall not die but live for you, my princess,' said the son of the King of Spain. And he kissed her little hand, got on his great white horse and rode away.

He rode and he rode and he rode, and his horse got tired. So, in a little wood, the prince dismounted and sat under an oak tree that his horse might rest, and drink from a spring that bubbled up out of the moss close by.

And whilst he was so sitting, the prince heard a kind of muffled shrieking, '*A-hoo, a-hoo*', and a flapping of wings above him; and looking up he saw a big white owl, with its head caught between two of the oak branches.

The prince quickly climbed the tree, pulled the branches apart, and freed the owl. The owl flopped to the ground, the prince came down from the tree, and when the owl had recovered his breath, he said, 'Prince, I am the king of the owls. Prince, I know who you are. I know that you seek the wine that gives youth. Of that wine there is but one bottle left in the world, and it is guarded, in the middle of a thicket of thorn trees, by a great monster that never sleeps. Take me up on your saddle, and I will show you the way to that thicket; and what a mere bird can do to help you overcome the monster, that I will do.'

'Thank you, king of the owls.'

'Prince, it is I who must thank *you*.'

Then the prince called his great white horse to him and jumped into the saddle. The king of the owls perched himself on the pommel, and away they rode over hill, over dale, till they came to the thicket of thorn trees. The thorn trees grew so close together that the great white horse couldn't get through them. So the prince left the horse and went into the thicket on foot, cutting his way through with his sword, and with the king of the owls perched on his shoulder.

In the midst of the thicket they came to a clearing. In the

clearing was a tree stump, and on the tree stump was the bottle of wine that gives youth: but coiled round that tree stump was the monster that never sleeps. The monster had a snake's head, a dragon's body, and a tail that ended in a sharp spike. When he saw the prince he lashed the ground with his spiked tail, tearing up the earth all round him; and then reared up his flat head, and hissed with a breath that blew the prince backwards. The prince had to crawl on hands and knees to get near that monster; but the king of the owls flew at the monster's head, and pecked and pecked, covering the great hissing mouth with his flapping wings. And the prince stood up, and thrust his sword here, there, and everywhere into the monster's writhing body.

For a long hour they fought, but at last the monster fell dead. The prince took the bottle of the wine that gives youth from the tree stump, and went out of the thicket with the king of the owls.

And when the prince was mounted on his horse again, the king of the owls said, 'Farewell, my prince! My debt of gratitude is paid. Now I can go back to my people. And we shall never meet again; no, never, never.'

The king of the owls flew away: the prince rode on and farther on. And he came to a rivulet. And on the edge of the rivulet was a wolf with his head caught in a trap. The prince jumped down, opened the trap, and freed the wolf.

And the wolf said, 'Thank you, my prince! I am the king of the wolves. I know who you are, and what you seek. Follow me, and I will lead you to the great wood where the ogre lives, the ogre who wears the breastplate that is proof against sword-thrust, bullet, and cannon-ball.'

'Thank you, my wolf! But if the ogre's breastplate is proof against my sword, how shall I kill him? Must I dodge behind him and strike him in the back?'

'No, my prince. In that breastplate there is a hole as big as your fist, just where the breastplate covers the ogre's heart. It is there that you must strike.'

So the wolf ran ahead and the prince rode behind, and they made such speed that it wasn't long before they came to the wood where the ogre lived. And out of the wood the ogre came rushing to meet them, waving a great club and roaring like a hundred demons. The prince leaped off his horse and ran to meet the ogre, dodging the blows from the club, and hacking and hewing with his sword. The horse charged at the ogre, kicking and biting. The wolf, with bared teeth, ran in to join the battle, snarling and tearing. But alas, the ogre was so huge that not one of them could reach above his knees, and many a bang they got from the ogre's club, and many a wound they gave the ogre's legs, but reach the breastplate that covered the ogre's chest, and the hole in the breastplate where it covered the ogre's heart, no, it seemed *that* they could never do.

'Gr-r-r!' snarled the wolf, with his teeth in one of the ogre's legs. '*E-e-e-e!*' whinnied the great white horse, with his teeth in the ogre's other leg. *Stab, stab,* went the prince's sword into the ogre's knees. *Thump, thump,* went the ogre's club threshing the ground, whilst the prince and the wolf and the great white horse dodged the blows as well as they could, but never drew back from the fight.

It seemed the fight might go on forever; but suddenly, with the wolf tugging at one leg, and the horse tugging at the other, they brought the ogre toppling to the ground, and the prince leaped onto the ogre's sprawled body and thrust his sword deep into the hole in the ogre's breastplate, the hole that lay over the ogre's heart.

That was the end of the ogre. The prince quickly stripped the ogre's dead body of his breastplate, and cut off the ogre's head. The head he strung on a rope at one side of the saddle, the breastplate he strung on a rope at the other side of the saddle, then he sprang up into the saddle himself.

'Thank you, my great white horse! Thank you, thank you, king of the wolves!'

And the king of the wolves said, 'Farewell, my prince. My

debt of gratitude is paid. Now I can go back to my people.
And we shall never meet again; no, never, never!'

The wolf galloped off, and the prince rode back to the king,
bringing him the wine that restores youth, the head of the
ogre, and the breastplate that was proof against sword-thrust,
bullet and cannon-ball.

And when he went with these things to the king, there was
the princess listening behind the door.

'King, I have brought you the three things you demanded
of me. And now I claim the hand of your daughter. Here is the
bottle of the wine that gives youth.'

The king was reluctant to drink that wine. Yes, he would
like to be young again—but then, he didn't want to lose the
princess.

He looked at the bottle. 'If this is not the true wine that
gives youth, I will have your head,' said he.

'Drink and see!'

The king put the bottle to his lips and drank. He drank,
drank, and the wine flowed like sunlight through all his limbs.
His white hair turned black, his old eyes sparkled, his withered
cheeks filled out, his stiff joints became supple—yes, he was
young again, young again! He laughed, he snapped his fingers,
he jumped about, he leaped off his throne and onto his throne
again, he danced round and round his throne. 'Young, young,
young!'

But still he didn't want to lose his daughter. He looked at
the ogre's head, he looked at the ogre's breastplate. 'But the
breastplate is too big!' said he. 'How can I wear a thing that
towers over me like a hill? And besides—how do I know that
it is proof against sword-thrust and bullet and cannon-ball?'

'Give me but twelve hours' grace,' said the prince, 'and I
will prove to you that the breastplate is all that I claim for it.'

'Very well,' said the king. 'But if it is not—I will have your
head!'

The prince took up the breastplate and went from the king's
presence. The princess, who had skipped away from behind

the door, met him in the garden. She didn't wait this time for
him to kiss her hand. She flung her arms round his neck and
kissed him on both cheeks. 'I love you, I love you!' she cried.
'If my father will not give me to you—we will run away
together!'

'The king must keep his royal word as all kings must,' said
the prince. He rode to the town and came to a smithy where a
blacksmith was hammering out horseshoes, and his twenty
apprentices were working at a forge.

'Blacksmith,' said the prince, 'can you make two breastplates, sizeable for a man to wear, out of this huge one?'

'Easily, my prince.'

'Then blacksmith, if you will make me, by tomorrow
morning, out of this huge breastplate, two breastplates sizeable
for a man to wear, and exactly alike, I will give you a thousand
gold pieces; and another thousand gold pieces I will divide
among your apprentices.'

'It shall be done, my prince.'

All that night the blacksmith and his twenty apprentices
worked at the forge, melting down the ogre's breastplate, and
making from it two breastplates exactly alike and sizeable for
a man to wear. When the prince came to the forge in the
morning, the two breastplates were ready. So the blacksmith
got his thousand gold pieces, and each of the apprentices got
fifty gold pieces; the prince put on one breastplate, and carrying the other, went back to the king.

'My king, I bring you two breastplates, proof against sword-
thrust, bullet or cannon-ball. Which will you have?'

'I will have the one you are wearing,' said the king. 'But
how do I know that it is proof against sword-thrust, bullet,
and cannon-ball?'

'King, draw your sword and strike at the breastplate I am
wearing. Strike hard, hard!'

The king drew his sword. He struck with all his might. The
sword could not pierce that breastplate.

'King, come closer, come closer! Take your two pistols,

set them against the breastplate I am wearing, and discharge them.'

The king ,with a pistol in each hand, set the muzzles against the breastplate and fired. The shots glanced harmlessly aside.

'King, order up your soldiers to discharge a cannon-shot at my breastplate.'

The king sent for his soldiers: they came dragging in a cannon. They aimed at the prince's breastplate and fired.

Bang, bang, bang! There was the prince tumbled to the ground.

'I knew it, I knew it!' cried the king. 'He has deceived me with his miserable breastplate!'

But the prince jumped up immediately. 'It was but the force of the blow,' said he, 'you see I am unhurt! King, I have given you the wine that restores youth, I have given you the ogre's head, and here I give you the breastplate that is proof against sword-thrust, bullet and cannon-ball. Give me now my princess!'

'Yes, I suppose you must have her,' said the king.

And after all what did it matter? The king was now young, he needn't live alone; he could marry again if it so pleased him. He found that he didn't really mind losing the princess. So he held a grand wedding for his daughter and the prince. And after the wedding the princess kissed her father, and set off for Spain with her husband.

And in Spain they lived happily ever after.

The Magic Wand

There was once a man who bought a fine big piece of ground, and on this piece of ground he planned to build a fine big house. So he called a builder to him, and showed him the plans of the house, and the builder called his workmen and began to build. But when the house was nearly finished the man found he hadn't any money left to pay for it. What was he to do? He felt desperate. He went out into the country and wandered about, groaning and beating his breast. 'Oh what a fool I've been! What a fool!'

And up out of the ground jumped a demon and said, 'Man, oh man, why do you groan and beat your breast?'

The man told him, and the demon said, 'If I may have your son when he's eighteen years old, I will give you now two million gold pieces.'

The man said, 'I haven't a son.'

'Never mind for that,' said the demon, '*If* you have one.' Done and done! The man laughed. He'd been married a long time and had no children. Was it likely now that he'd have a son? So he signed a contract that the demon drew up, and hurried off home with two million gold pieces.

All went merrily. The house was finished, the builder was paid, and the man and his wife moved into the new house. A fine grand house it was: they lived in style, they had plenty of gold left, but—there you are—a day came when the man's wife gave birth to a baby son.

They christened the baby Benedict; they loved him dearly, and the man tried not to think about the contract he had signed with the demon; but, as Benedict grew, the man thought of that contract more and more: it haunted his days, it haunted his nights, and he became sad as sad.

But he wouldn't tell Benedict why he was sad, though the boy often asked him.

Now on the day that Benedict was eighteen he found his father in tears. So what did that lad do? He bought a pistol, and asked his father to come for a walk in the wood. And when they had come to the middle of the wood, Benedict took the pistol out of his pocket and said, 'Father, if you won't tell me what is troubling you, I shall shoot you, and then I shall shoot myself.'

So then the man wept even more bitterly, and told Benedict about the demon.

Pooh! Benedict wasn't afraid of the demon! He gave his father the pistol to keep, and set off at once for the demon's house. Mind you, he didn't know where that house was; but he thought if he walked straight on, he'd come to it sooner or later. So, after walking for a while, he saw an old woman at the side of the road, stooping over a pile of sticks. The old woman was trying to tie the sticks into a bundle; but her poor old hands were shaking; as fast as she picked up one stick she dropped another, and the rope she was trying to tie round them got all twisted and tangled.

'Oh deary me, oh deary me!' whimpered the old woman. 'What can a poor body do? These sticks are bewitched, I do think!'

'Why granny,' says Benedict, 'sit you down and rest on this grass bank. I'll soon make the sticks into a bundle for you!'

And make them into a bundle he very soon did, and tied them up good and proper. And then says he, 'Granny, if you're going my way, take my arm, I'll carry the bundle.'

'Oh, how kind!' said the old woman.

So they walked on together for a mile or two, Benedict with the bundle of sticks slung across his back, and the old woman, with her arm through his, hobbling at his side.

And then they came to a little hut, and the old woman said, 'This is where I live, and if you'll step inside, my lad, you shall have a cup of milk and a bite of bread . . . and may be something else, yes, may be something else!'

Benedict was quite hungry by this time, and he was glad enough to get something to eat and drink, so he went in with the old woman. He put the bundle of sticks down on the hearth, and the old woman set milk and bread before him. And when he had eaten, she said, 'My lad, do you know who I am?'

'Nay granny,' said Benedict, 'how should I?'

'And did you carry my bundle and give me an arm out of the kindness of your heart, not looking for any reward?'

'Why of course, granny!'

'Ah ha!' said the old woman, 'but I'm a fairy. I know where you're going, and why you're going. And here is something for you.'

And she gave him a little white wand.

'You have but to strike with this wand and say to it 'do'—whatever you wish done, and the wand will do it. So now never mind thanking me, but be off with you. Take the thirteenth turning to the left and you'll come to the demon's house. And you may be sure my blessing goes with you!'

So Benedict said good-bye to the old fairy and set off again, took the thirteenth turning to the left, and came to the demon's house. The door of the house was open, and he went in and found the demon in the kitchen, putting on his boots.

'So here you are,' said the demon, 'I was just getting into my boots to come and fetch you.'

'Well now I've come, give me something to eat,' said Benedict, 'for I'm hungry.'

The demon set food before him, Benedict ate up everything and asked for more.

'What, *more!*' said the demon.

'Yes, a lot more,' said Benedict. 'I've not done growing yet, and I have to keep my strength up.'

Benedict and the demon from *The Magic Wand*

So the demon set more food before him, and Benedict ate it all up and asked for more.

'No, I shan't give you any more,' said the demon. 'I can't afford it.'

'Well then,' said Benedict, 'give me some work to do, for I'm not used to sitting idle.'

Now behind the demon's house was a forest, and the demon gave Benedict an axe and a tinder-box and took him into this forest. He told him to cut down a tree or two and make some charcoal.

'All right, I'll do that,' said Benedict. And the demon went away and left him.

Then Benedict went from tree to tree, striking them with

his wand and bidding them be cut down. And it wasn't long before he had all the trees in the forest lying flat. And then he struck them again and bade them become charcoal: and they became charcoal. There was nothing of the forest left now, but black mounds piled on black mounds.

So Benedict went back into the demon's house. 'I've finished the task you gave me,' said he. 'And now let me have something to eat, for I'm hungry.'

'Oh, oh, oh!' said the demon. 'You'll ruin me completely! I gave you enough to fill a giant only an hour ago.'

'I'm a growing lad,' said Benedict, 'I can't grow on air. But if you're not satisfied, give me back the contract my father signed, and I'll be off this minute.'

'No, I won't do that!' said the demon. And he brought Benedict some more food. 'But I don't believe you can have finished your work so quickly,' said he. And off with him to the forest to see what Benedict had done.

Left alone, Benedict touched his plate of meat and his jug of beer with the wand. 'Vanish meat, vanish beer,' said he. And immediately there was the plate scraped clean and the jug empty.

Very soon after that, the demon came back. He was screaming. 'All my forest burnt down! All my forest burnt down!'

'Well, if you're not satisfied,' said Benedict, 'give me back the contract, and I'll leave you.'

'I won't, I *won't*, I WON'T give you back the contract,' screamed the demon.

'Then give me more work, for I can't sit here idle.'

The demon was trying to think of some task that Benedict couldn't do, and at last he had an idea. He took Benedict out and showed him two big pools. In one the water was clear, and it was full of fish; but the other pool was filled with mud.

'Dry up that muddy pool and turf it over,' said the demon. 'And if you haven't done that in an hour's time, my lad, it'll be the worse for you!'

Then the demon went back into his house. He was chuckling, because the muddy pool had no bottom, and the mud in
it kept rising from a swamp in the other world: it could never
be dried up.

Benedict was chuckling too. He struck the two pools with
the rod, and told the rod what he wanted. Hey presto! There
was the clear pool dried up and turfed over, and there were all
the fishes floundering in the muddy one.

In an hour the demon came out. When he saw what
Benedict had done he danced with rage. 'Wretch! Pig!
Scoundrel!' he screamed. 'It wasn't that pool I told you to
empty!'

'Well, if you're not satisfied, you know what to do,' said
Benedict. 'Give me back the contract.'

'Never, never, never!' screamed the demon.

'Well then I'm hungry, give me some food.'

'You'll ruin me!' cried the demon. 'We only cook on
Saturdays, and you've emptied the larder already! Can you
cook, villain?'

'Of course I can cook. I can do anything.'

'Well then, cook what you must with what you can find.'

So Benedict went into the kitchen, lit the stove, bade the
wand bring him some flour and some fat, and began to make
pastry.

And as he's busy with his hands in the dough, the six little
sons of the demon come running into the kitchen, tugging at
his coat and clamouring:

'Benedict, make me an oil cake!'

'Benedict, make me a lardy cake!'

'Benedict, make me a pancake!'

'Go away,' says Benedict, 'you're annoying me.'

But the six little demons wouldn't go away, they went on
tugging at Benedict's coat and clamouring. So then Benedict
gets really vexed, and seizes them up one after the other and
bundles them into the oven—all but the youngest and he
escapes and rushes off to tell his father.

The demon leaps in, raging. He snatches the children out of the oven and shouts at Benedict: 'What are you thinking of, you—you—*you!* You do us nothing but harm!'

Says Benedict, 'Not satisfied? Then give me the contract.'

'Take it and be off!' shouts the demon.

And he throws the contract at Benedict's head.

So Benedict put the contract in his pocket and walked off laughing.

He walked all the rest of the day. In the evening he came to a village and looked round for somewhere to sleep. There's an old castle near by, and folk tell him it's haunted. 'Never mind for that,' thinks Benedict, 'it'll do to pass the night in.' So he goes to the castle and it's all dark and empty. He gropes his way to the kitchen, strikes the hearth with his wand, and orders a fire. There, now the fire's blazing. He strikes a table with the wand and orders food and drink and candles. There, he has all that. So he makes a good meal. Then he blows out the candles and curls himself up by the hearth to sleep.

At midnight he's woken by a clattering of feet. In come twelve demons and begin to dance. 'Go away,' says Benedict, 'you're disturbing me.' But the demons won't go away. So he strikes eleven of them with his wand, and they fall dead. There's only one demon left now, and that one's hiding in a corner. And it's the very demon with whom Benedict's father had made the contract. He's whimpering now, thinking he's going to be killed.

'Stop squealing!' says Benedict. 'I'm not going to do anything to *you*, because I've lodged in your house and eaten your food. But why do you come here?'

So then the demon said that he and his fellows had been coming every night for the past fifty years to safeguard a treasure that was hidden in a cellar under the castle. If they could safeguard it for a hundred years it would be theirs. And it was from this very treasure, he said, that he had taken the two million gold pieces he had given to Benedict's father.

'And now,' says the demon, cheering up a bit, 'since you're not going to kill me, in another fifty years all that treasure will be mine.'

'Oh will it?' says Benedict. 'You just show me that treasure.'

The demon didn't want to, but he must, because Benedict threatened him with the wand. So he led the way down to the cellar, and showed Benedict a barrel full of gold and a barrel full of silver, buried up to their lids in the earth. Benedict touched the barrels with his wand, and they rose out of the earth.

'Now,' says Benedict to the demon, 'up with those barrels, one on each shoulder.'

'They're too heavy,' says the demon, shedding tears.

'Up with them,' says Benedict. 'Or shall my wand tickle you?'

'No, no, no!' sobs the demon. And there he is, with a barrel on each shoulder, staggering up out of the cellar and into the castle court. He wanted to put the barrels down then, but Benedict said, 'No such thing!' And he made the demon carry those barrels all the way to his father's house.

When they got to the house the demon set the barrels down at the door. 'I'm aching all over,' says he, 'and aren't I to have one little bit of the treasure?'

'Not one little bit,' says Benedict. 'Do you think I'm going to reward you for causing my father eighteen years of misery? You be off with you. And if you ever come troubling us again, you know what to expect. My wand has killed eleven demons: it can kill a twelfth just as easily.'

The demon ran off then. He was glad enough to go. Benedict went in to his parents.

'Oh, oh, oh! We thought the demon must have killed you!'

'Not he!' says Benedict. 'He's gone for good. And I've brought you something to put on the fire.'

Then he gave his father the contract. And his father burned it.

'I've brought you something else,' says Benedict. And he took them out and showed them the two barrels of treasure standing in the doorway.

So, if they were rich before, they were richer now. And they lived in peace and happiness ever after.

The Nine White Sheep

There was a girl called Milia, and she had nine little brothers. Their father and mother were both dead; but they weren't poor, they were rich. They lived in a big house with a lovely garden; they had an old nurse to take care of them, and good kind servants to see to the house and garden.

There were a great many birds in the garden, and Milia fed them all and was fond of them all. But her greatest friend amongst them was a red and blue parrot. This parrot could talk, and he told Milia a lot of wonderful and amusing things. But sometimes he would grow sad and say, 'Ah Milia, if only I were a human being like you! There was a time when, a time when . . .'

'A time when what?' asked Milia.

But then the parrot drew the lids up over his eyes and said, 'Never mind, never mind. Least said the soonest mended.'

Now on Milia's fifteenth birthday, her nine little brothers went into the woods to pick wild strawberries for her. They went farther than they had ever been before, and they came to a little house. And they were thirsty, so they knocked at the door of the little house to ask for a drink of water. And who should open the door but a hideous witch, with a tongue wrapped seven times round her body.

Oh! Oh! The little boys were frightened. They thought they would run away, but the witch began to sob: 'Now there it is, there it is, what's a poor old body to do if her looks scare away everyone that comes to call on her? A poor old body can't help being ugly, can she?'

And the tears went drip, drip, drip, down the witch's hideous wrinkled cheeks.

So then the little boys, who had been brought up very nicely by their old nurse, felt ashamed, and the eldest said, 'If you please, ma'am, we knocked at your door because we're thirsty, and we thought perhaps you might give us a drink of water.'

The witch asked the little boys to come inside. She gave them each a glass of water, and patted their heads and stroked their cheeks, and told them what handsome little fellows they were. The little boys didn't much like the way she was going on; but they remembered their manners, and put up with it. They drank the water, placed the glasses carefully back on the table, said 'Thank you, ma'am', and thought to go, when the witch said, 'What! Go without paying a poor old body? Oh no, you can't do that!'

'If you please, ma'am,' said the eldest little boy, 'we haven't any money. But when we get home we will ask our sister for some and bring it to you.'

'Money!' says the old witch. 'What do I want with money? It's a little husband *I'm* wanting. Now which of you is going to be my little husband?'

And she leered at them most horribly.

Oh! Oh! Oh! Now the little boys were really terrified.

The eldest just managed to stammer out, 'If you please, ma'am, we'll—we'll ask our sister,' and then they took to their heels. And the witch called after them, 'I shall come tomorrow morning for your sister's answer.'

When the little boys got home they were crying. They told Milia about the witch, and Milia said, 'What an idea! She shan't have any one of you!'

So then the little boys cheered up.

The next morning—*knock! knock!*—there was the witch come for her answer.

The little boys tried to hide behind Milia; the eldest held on to her skirt, and the rest were in a row behind him, each one clinging to another. Milia spread out her arms to protect them, and the witch says, 'Well, which boy am I to have?'

'You're not having any one of them,' says Milia. 'Go away please.'

'Oh, so it's go away, is it?' yelled the witch.

And she ran out, screaming.

Crash! The earth heaved, the sky thundered: the house, the garden, the old nurse, the good kind servants—all vanished. Milia was flung to the ground; she struggled up and looked round her. She was standing in the middle of a flat grassy plain—and where were her little brothers?

Baa-aa! Baa-aa! They were there behind her. But those nine little brothers had become nine white sheep.

'Oh my little brothers, my little brothers!'

Baa-aa! Baa-aa! They clustered round her: she fondled their heads, and wept.

But then, what use in weeping? What had happened, had happened, and she must make the best of it. The sheep grazed on the flat grassy plain, Milia tended them, and talked to them, and played with them. It wasn't such a bad life once she got used to it. She found a pile of old wood and built a hut for nights and rainy weather; and three times a day her friend, the blue and red parrot, came carrying food for her in a little basket.

'We're quite happy, aren't we, Milia?' says the parrot.

'Why yes, my parrot, I do believe we're quite happy,' says Milia.

But when the witch learned that Milia was happy, she was furious. So one noonday, when it was very hot, Milia felt sleepy, oh so sleepy, and she went into the hut. The nine white sheep were grazing close—they were quite safe: yes, Milia would just take a little nap. And she shut her eyes. Then came the witch, softly, softly, round the corner of the hut, and blew with her breath. A grey fog covered the plain: and when the fog lifted, the nine white sheep were gone.

Milia woke and came out of the hut: the grassy plain stretched away on all sides of her, empty, empty. 'Oh my little brothers, my little brothers, my nine little white sheep— where are you?'

No answer.

And Milia sat down and wept, wept, wept, as if her heart would break.

Peck, peck, peck! There was the blue and red parrot pecking at her sleeve.

'Milia, silly girl, get up, get up! Is this a time to sit and cry? The witch has taken the nine white sheep and put them in her barn. Oh yes, she will feed them well; but when they are fat enough she will eat them. If we are to save them, we must hurry. Come, I will show you the way to the witch's house!'

Away they went, the parrot flying low, Milia running at his side. And when they came near to the witch's house, the parrot said, 'Now listen to me, Milia. You must accept nothing from the witch, neither food, nor drink, nor any pretty thing. If you do, she will change you into a statue, and then you are lost forever. Ask only a corner to sleep in, and that she will grant. For she will want to keep you.'

'My parrot, I will do as you say.'

'Then knock at the door, Milia.'

Rat, tat, tat! Milia knocked; the parrot flew up onto the roof; the witch opened the door.

'Ah! It is the little sister seeking her brothers! They are safe and happy, my pretty, eating well and sleeping soft. Come in, come in, little darling! Here, you shall eat a morsel of this nice cake, and drink a glass of this delicious wine!'

'Thank you, madam, but I have neither hunger nor thirst.'

'What, after your long walk! Surely you must be tired?'

'Yes, madam, I am rather tired. I would be grateful if you have any little corner where I might lie down and sleep.'

'As you please, my lovely one,' said the witch. But she thought, 'I shan't let her escape, the little hussy!'

So there she is now, the old hag, rummaging in a chest, and bringing out one pretty thing after another to tempt Milia. 'See now this pretty diamond ring: let me put it on your finger! And here is a gold collar for your white neck! And oh my! Look at this silk dress that shimmers and changes colour like the sky at dawn! Take them, put them on, my darling! It shall never be said that a guest comes to my house without carrying away some mark of my bounty!'

But Milia said, 'What should a poor girl do with silk robes and gold collars? No, no, I am best dressed as I am.'

'As you please, my darling,' said the witch. But she thought, 'I'll get her yet!'

So then Milia lay down in a corner by the hearth, and the witch went upstairs to her bed, and lay awake planning how she would trap Milia into accepting something in the morning. But by and by she fell asleep, and snored loudly.

Then the parrot came and tapped at the kitchen window.

'Milia, Milia, are you waking?'

'Yes, my parrot.'

'Then open the window, Milia, and let me in.'

Milia opened the window very quietly. The parrot flew in. He had a great sharp knife in his beak.

'Milia, take this knife and kill the witch whilst she sleeps.'

'Oh no, my parrot, I couldn't!'

'What, not to save your brothers?'

'Oh my parrot, I cannot kill! I cannot!'

'Then I must do it myself,' said the parrot. And he flew up to the witch's room and cut her throat with the great sharp knife.

Yes, the parrot flew up. But what came down? A handsome lad, no less. And the handsome lad was carrying the witch's chemise.

'Milia, I am your parrot. Milia, the witch who changed me into a bird because I wouldn't marry her, is dead. Milia read what is written in gold letters on the hem of this chemise.'

Milia took the chemise and read:

'You who wear me, do but say
What you wish, and I obey.'

'Yes, Milia,' said the handsome lad, 'all the witch's power was in this garment. Now put it on, and her power is yours. We can rescue your brothers, Milia!'

So Milia put on the chemise, and she and the handsome lad ran to the barn. There were the nine white sheep, huddled in a corner, and very miserable. But when they saw Milia they leaped up and skipped for joy.

Then Milia said, 'Chemise, chemise, let these sheep become human beings.'

Immediately the sheep's white woolly coats disappeared. Their horns fell off, their hoofs changed into hands and feet. And Milia, with tears of joy running down her cheeks, was hugging and kissing her nine little brothers.

And the handsome lad said, 'Milia, there are more unhappy people enchanted in this house.' And he led her to a long room full of statues: the statue of a king, the statue of a queen, the statues of lords and ladies.

'Chemise, chemise,' said Milia, 'I wish that these statues come alive.'

And immediately the long room was filled with happy people, crowding round Milia, thanking her, thanking her, blessing her, praising her, offering her gold and silver, offering her castles and towns, offering their very selves to serve her for ever.

But Milia shook her head. No, no, she would accept nothing. Hadn't she the magic chemise to give her all she wanted? So she bade the chemise call up out of the earth beautiful gold carriages drawn by prancing horses to take the people back to their homes. And they drove away blessing her.

'But you,' said Milia to the handsome lad, 'where is your home?'

'Ah Milia,' said he, 'I think my home is with you. If you can love me?'

'Yes, I can love you, my parrot,' laughed Milia. 'For without your help I should have lost all.'

'And now chemise, chemise,' said she, 'I wish for a coach to carry us home. And let our home be as it was, our beautiful house with its garden and orchard, and let our good old nurse and our kind servants be waiting to welcome us.'

No sooner said than done. Up from the ground rose a magnificent coach, drawn by eight prancing horses, with a coachman in a cocked hat holding the reins, and two little lackeys to open the coach doors and help them in. Away they drove, merrily, merrily, and came to the place where Milia had tended her nine white sheep on the great plain. As you may well guess, the plain had disappeared. There was the lovely garden, there was the big beautiful house, there on the steps before the door stood the dear old nurse to welcome them in.

So Milia married the handsome lad, and they all lived happily, happily: so happily that it seemed to Milia there was nothing more the chemise could do for her.

But there was something Milia could do for the chemise: and that was to wash it. So she washed it and spread it out in the sun to dry. And a tramp came along and thought, 'Aha! That chemise would do nicely for my missus!' And he snatched it up and ran off with it. Maybe he could read what was written on it; maybe he couldn't. Maybe the chemise brought him and his missus a fortune; maybe it didn't.

At any rate, neither the tramp nor the chemise was ever heard of again.